THE **FORCES**
OF **FREEDOM**
IN **SPAIN**, 1974–1979

THE FORCES OF FREEDOM IN SPAIN, 1974–1979

A Personal Account
SAMUEL D. EATON

HOOVER INSTITUTION PRESS
Stanford University, Stanford, California

*The Hoover Institution on War, Revolution and Peace, founded at
Stanford University in 1919 by the late President Herbert Hoover,
is an interdisciplinary research center for advanced study on
domestic and international affairs in the twentieth century. The views
expressed in its publications are entirely those of the authors
and do not necessarily reflect the views of the staff, officers,
or Board of Overseers of the Hoover Institution.*

Hoover Press Publication 245

© 1981 by the Board of Trustees of the
  Leland Stanford Junior University
All rights reserved
International Standard Book Number: 0–8179–7452–0
Library of Congress Catalog Card Number: 80–83831
Printed in the United States of Ameria

Design by P. Kelley Baker

To my wife Mechi, with love, and my special appreciation for her stimulating company in so many parts of this planet.

CONTENTS

Foreword. xi

Prologue: Assignment to Spain xv

CHAPTERS
1 Franco's Last Two Years 1
2 The United States Between Past and Future. 12
3 The New King. 29
4 The King Gambles. 41
5 Could Euphoria Last? 56
6 Eurocommunism and Eurosocialism, Spanish Style. . 71
7 Basque Autonomy and the Dilemmas
       Terrorism Spawns. 85
8 Suárez Seeks and Obtains a New Mandate. 96
9 An Active Spanish Foreign Policy under the King . . 108
10 The United States and the Emerging
       Spanish Democracy 116
11 The Forces of Freedom in Spain:
       Three Scenarios for the Future 133

APPENDIXES

A   Chronology of Main Events 147
B   Principal Personalities 153
C   Spanish Constitutions. 159

Selected Bibliography 165

Index 167

ILLUSTRATIONS

_____

These illustrations will be found in a group following page 16

1. Ships under construction at San Carlos Shipyard, Cadiz
2. Franco at diplomatic ceremony during his last year
3. Mechi receives a guest at Don Ramón de la Cruz 3
4. Meeting of the Spanish-American Council under the Treaty of Friendship
5. King Juan Carlos and Queen Sofía
6. Prime Minister Adolfo Suárez
7. The first Basque parliament under the 1978 Constitution
8. The Mayor of Oñate makes a point

FOREWORD

This book has two topics: first, the political transition in Spain from forty years of authoritarianism under Franco to a fascinating and perhaps instructive effort to achieve stable democracy under a constitutional monarch, King Juan Carlos I; and second, the foreign relations of the United States with Spain during the first years of the transition. It is a personal account, born of personal witness. The reader will find here my individual view of what happened and why, of issues and of personalities, of lessons that may be learned and of questions that remain, drawn from my own experience in Spain from 1974 to 1978 and in the Foreign Service for over thirty years, and matured by subsequent study.

In Spain I had the great good fortune of being deputy chief of mission and minister counselor of embassy from June 1974 to August 1978. Because of two changes of ambassador in this period and also frequent travel by the ambassadors to the United States, I was in charge of the United States Mission to Spain—that is, all United States government operations there—for a total of thirteen of my fifty months' assignment to Madrid. It was part of my job to make a special effort, throughout my time in Spain, to analyze and understand what was going on politically and economically as it affected United States interests, and to know and understand the motives and actions of the principal leaders of Spain.

In the Foreign Service I have served primarily in South America and Washington, but also have had in addition to one tour in the Far East, the one tour of Europe that is the principal subject of this book. My career has included lengthy periods of work in macroeconomics, economic development, and commercial relations, and also considerable time at political analysis and in management functions. I have done some consular work. My college training was primarily in history and government, and I have always felt strongly the importance of integrating political and economic analysis— an approach to the understanding of events and issues that is all too infrequent in both academe and the diplomatic service. My work in economic development has whetted my interest in a broader view of development issues, to include the political and the social as well as the economic.

It is against this background that I have set down in the following pages an account of the historic and at times dramatic events in Spain over the past five years, and of the role of the United States there in that period. I have interspersed this account with, I hope, enough personal anecdotes to add a bit of life to the history and opinion that are this work's main purpose.

A Foreign Service officer passes much of his career observing and writing. He writes telegrams, analytical pieces, and policy papers in such numbers that they are but a blur in his memory. But he seldom writes books. There is not time until his career is over or unless he is given a sabbatical, as I fortunately was in the 1978/79 academic year. And anyway, by tradition, he has a certain reticence about going public. His skills, and customs, are more attuned to the needs, workings, and necessary confidentialities of the official foreign affairs community.

It has thus been a new, stimulating, and even rather exciting experience to produce a book. It has been all the more stimulating and exciting because it has permitted—indeed required—further research and reflection on the fascinating process of the Spanish democratic transition that I had the good fortune personally to witness.

If the end product turns out to be attractive to the reader, that is certainly mainly because of the interest of the subject itself. To the extent that I have done justice to that subject, I owe much to my many friends and colleagues in Spain who, during the fifty months that I lived and served there, helped me know and understand what was happening. I am also beholden to academic and diplomatic colleagues who, after my writing had begun, took the time to read, and offer constructive criticism on, my manuscript at various stages. They, of course, bear no responsibility for the final work's shortcomings. Nor does my government, for this is a personal work. Those colleagues included Professors Charles Larsen, Larry Schrader, Stanley Payne, Richard Herr, Robert Wesson, William Salisbury, Edward Le Fevour, and Howard Wiarda; Dr. Easton Rothwell; Ambassadors Nathaniel Davis, Robert Woodward, and Willard Beaulac; and Ambassador (and President of Mills College) Barbara White.

I am reminded as I write this last name that I am, additionally, much indebted to Mills College for offering me such a congenial atmosphere in which to write.

Finally, the quality of the finished work has certainly been improved by the editorial criticism of, first Mrs. Florence Myer, and then, especially, Mr. J. M. B. Edwards.

But all this, by itself, would not have been sufficient. One also needs stimulating, understanding, and sympathetic companionship to produce a work of this nature. My wife has given me just such companionship in most generous measure. Her maiden name, Mercedes Herrera del Carpio, is only a minor indicator of the contagious and supportive enthusiasm she had, and has, for Spain, its history, its current experience, its future, its simple being— which are so much a part of her own being.

S.D.E.

PROLOGUE
ASSIGNMENT
TO SPAIN

My wife, Mechi, sank slowly to the floor in disbelief at what I was telling her over the telephone from the Department of State. It was the afternoon before the packers were to come. It was also just ten days before we were to depart for Brasilia, where I was to be deputy chief of mission. All preparations had been made. Books, furniture, and all other items had been carefully separated and designated, part for shipment to Brasilia, part for storage in Washington until our ultimate return. Reservations had been made. Tickets were in hand. I was spending my mornings reacquainting myself with Portuguese at the Foreign Service Institute, as more than twenty years had passed since I last used that language, during our first assignment to Brazil. My afternoons I was spending at the Office of Brazilian Affairs, in the Department of State, familiarizing myself further with the principal issues in relations between the United States and Brazil. On this particular Tuesday afternoon in March I had just returned from a meeting at the Treasury Department, where we discussed Brazilian shoe exports, when I received a telephone call that abruptly changed our plans.

On that same afternoon my wife was having a cup of tea with a friend and contemplating with reluctant resignation the prospect of yet another posting in Latin America after so much concentration on that area over such a long period of time. It was not that we did not like Brazilians or were not interested in Brazil. Our memories of Brazilian friends from our assignment in Rio in the early 1950s were among the pleasantest of our Foreign Service career. And professionally the assignment was excellent. The country was important and would be more so in the future. The job was a top one. Moreover, I would be working directly under Ambassador John Crimmins, one of our finest career professionals and also a good friend. It was just that the issues and surroundings were so familiar. We had gone stale. We badly needed a change to stimulate us anew and to broaden our perspectives. We had always wanted at least one assignment in Europe, and were convinced that this should be the time for it: it made sense for us psychologically, and also for the Foreign Service in terms of my present and future professional effectiveness. After that one assignment to Europe we would be happy to return to Latin America, where we felt very much at home, with renewed enthusiasm and expanded background.

It so happened that Secretary of State Henry Kissinger agreed—at least philosophically—and precisely at that time took a general action on the assignment of Foreign Service personnel that changed our lives with dramatic suddenness. It was certainly not that he had me in mind as an individual. It was simply that during the recent meeting of foreign ministers of the hemisphere in Mexico City he had been unfavorably impressed by the parochial viewpoints of the United States Foreign Service officers who had done the preparatory work. It was naturally—almost inevitably—so. Most of these officers had had very little experience outside of Latin American affairs. The system was the cause. The regional geographic bureaus had a strong, and generally commanding, say on assignments; they tended to request the people they knew, reject the people they didn't, and treasure those with local experience and proven language ability. But the cost was narrowness of perspective and, over time, boredom with the repetitiveness of the issues dealt with. I myself had long argued as much in my own case, but to no avail, while I sought an out-of-area assignment. This Secretary Kissinger saw in Mexico City, and quickly did something about it in a generic way that, in the end, affected me individually exactly as I would have wished.

In the end, I say, because the process took some time to play out, and was not without its uncertainties and minor traumas along the way.

What the secretary did was to issue an order that, with few exceptions, all or at least a high percentage of all Foreign Service officers who had not had recent assignments outside their geographic area of specialty should have out-of-area assignments on their next transfer. The order was called the Global Outlook Program and was quickly dubbed GLOP. Soon it would be the fashion in the Foreign Service to be "glopped," and the stories of gloppers and gloppees were many. This order had come out the week before our date with the packers and two weeks before our scheduled departure for Brasilia. I had talked about it generally during lunch on that signal March Tuesday with the member of the National Security Staff concerned with Latin American affairs, but I had no idea at the time that it could affect me; after all, my assignment had already been made, and I was practically on the plane. Thus it was that at about 3:30 on this Tuesday afternoon I received a call from State Department Personnel. The conversation went something like this:

"Sam, you've heard of GLOP, haven't you?"

"Yes, vaguely."

"We think it probably affects you."

"Do you realize that the packers are coming tomorrow, and we are scheduled to get on the plane in ten days?"

"Oh! No, we didn't realize it had gone that far. I'd better check to make sure it applies to you. But I should warn you it probably does. We are stopping somebody in his car on the way from Brussels to Switzerland to tell him his transfer is not going to be that simple. He will more likely have to fly or swim to the next post rather than drive."

"You'd better find out quickly whether GLOP applies to me, because I have to tell the packers something this afternoon."

"I understand. We'll take it to the director general and be back to you as quickly as we can."

After this conversation I sat back for a moment to think. I concluded it would be difficult for the director general of the Foreign Service to reach a decision on this specific case before Security Storage, the moving company, closed for the afternoon. Therefore I called Security Storage, told them the circumstances, and suggested they postpone sending the packers for a few days. Their response, from long experience with the Foreign Service, was one of complete understanding. They had seen this sort of thing happen many times. There was no problem. I should just let them know when the packing should be rescheduled—and for where.

I called Mechi to tell her that everything was up in the air and that in any event the packers would not be coming the next day. Thereupon, in a state of shock, she quietly slipped to a sitting position on the floor—without, I am told, spilling a drop of tea.

In the old days, when the Foreign Service was less stodgy, perhaps less efficient, but certainly blessed with a greater sense of humor, it had the quaint idea that every Foreign Service officer should make his annual submission of preferences for his next assignment on April 1. The date immediately conveyed the essense of the process: you may—in fact, are required to—state your preferences; but don't be so foolish as to think they are overriding. Obviously not everybody can go where he wants to. Worldwide availability is one of the Service's basic tenets; it takes into account the officer's preferences—to be realistic, the more so the closer he is to the decision-making people—but in the end it will assign him where its needs dictate.

More recently, in order to even out the personnel office's annual workload, assignment preferences are submitted in the month of the officer's birth date—a more efficient but, I am sure, less apposite procedure. Moreover, considerable effort is made to provide all officers with current information on job vacancies, and to consult with them during the six months prior to their new assignments regarding which of those vacancies most interests them. However, I would guess that for most officers the results of the assignment process still appear closer to an April Fool's Day prank than a birthday present.

The problem is in part that preferences just naturally tend to concentrate on a relatively few posts, while all posts must be staffed; in part that no one can know or predict in advance exactly what the next post will be like and how much he will like or dislike it for one reason or another; and in part that the new approach tends to raise expectations unduly. It places the emphasis a bit too much on the officer's convenience, when the officer and his family cannot entirely predict their convenience, and a bit too little on the concept of worldwide service—a concept that is essential to the effective functioning of the Foreign Service and that should be a major source of pride to it.

My own experience with the Foreign Service assignment process over thirty years has had its ups and downs, and has not lacked its moments of considerable humor. Certainly, I have not always gone just where I wanted to go. But I could not and should not have expected to, and on the whole there has been a reasonable balance between my personal desires and needs on the one hand and the requirements of the service on the other. We both should be satisfied, I think. Certainly I am satisfied at this point, particularly when I take into account Secretary Kissinger's latter-day intervention and its end result—the four extraordinary years in Spain—that are the main subject of this book.

Twenty-three of my first twenty-five years in the Foreign Service were spent either working in Latin America, or dealing primarily with Latin American affairs from Washington. It was with this background that in 1973 I went to Foreign Service Personnel and to the director general of the Foreign Service, Nathaniel Davis, to make my point that it really was time for me to receive new stimulation and a broadening of perspective by being assigned to Europe.

Personnel at first held out some hope, saying that the job of deputy chief of mission in Madrid would be opening up and that I would be one of the logical candidates. But the Madrid job did not open up in 1973, and toward the middle of the year Jack Kubisch, the new assistant secretary for Latin American affairs, asked what I wanted and offered to help me get it. I said I very much wanted to go to Europe for reasons I considered persuasive from both a personal and a Foreign Service point of view. In response to his further questioning, I said that, in any event, whether or not I went to Europe I would prefer a deputy-chief-of-mission job in a large, active, important embassy to an ambassadorship in a small, inactive post. Jack said he would do what he could and later proposed that I become deputy chief of mission in Buenos Aires, the appointment to be effective in November or December when a new ambassador was to go to Argentina. Mechi and I were both pleased with this prospect. If we could not go to Europe, Argentina was as good an alternative as one could imagine; therefore, for three or four months we assumed we would be off to Buenos Aires for Christmas. Then, one morning in early December, I read in the *Washington Post* the name of the new appointee as ambassador in Argentina. It was not the name that had been anticipated, and the new man had his own selection for deputy. Christmas in Buenos Aires was not to be for us.

The next proposal early in 1974 was Brasilia—a challenging post, but not Europe. I agreed to go and we were all but on the plane when, as I have recounted, Personnel called on that April Tuesday to say that I looked like a gloppee.

After work that night, I went home convinced it would take at least a day or two for Personnel and the director general to decide whether I was really to be glopped or not. But, to my surprise, Nat Davis called me at about 7:30 P.M. to say that, while we should keep the Brasilia option open for the time being, he thought I was subject to GLOP, he knew I wanted a European assignment, and he would try to find one for me.

In our library, among books neatly divided between those marked for Brasilia and those marked for storage, Mechi and I reflected on what had happened that day. We were torn between happiness at the possibility of at last going to Europe and a degree of pessimism born of past disappointments and the understanding that no assignment as deputy chief of mission could be certain until the ambassador whose deputy you would be agreed.

Over the next few days I explored the prospects further. As part of keeping the Brasilia option open I continued to study Portuguese, though with a considerable decline in enthusiasm. Four European posts were mentioned to me as possibilities: Madrid again, Athens, Brussels, and Belgrade. They were all attractive to us, but Madrid was the most attractive and Nat Davis said he would work specifically for that.

But there was a catch. Admiral Horacio Rivero, a strong-willed former deputy chief of naval operations, was ambassador to Spain; and at the end of 1973 he had persuaded the Foreign Service to go against usual practice by elevating his political counselor to the position of deputy chief of mission. Now, however, GLOP had entered the picture. The political counselor was on home leave, and since he had already had five years in Spain it did not seem in the spirit of GLOP for him to be returned to Madrid for an indefinite further period. Nat Davis put this point up to Ambassador Rivero and recommended me as his new deputy. Ambassador Rivero was not at all pleased by this turn of events. He had selected his man; he knew him; he didn't know me; he wanted him; and he thought that should be sufficient.

Thus began a period of negotiation that extended over six weeks.

As time passed with no decision, I went to New York for a special session of the United Nations, while Mechi continued trying to rent our house on the assumption that we would actually go abroad somewhere sometime. After I had been at the United Nations for a few days, she called to tell me that she had found just the right couple. I said fine, and that she could make a 90 percent commitment to rent it to them in a month. She should not go further than that because, after all, we were not absolutely sure we would really be going abroad. That night she called again and put the prospective renter on the phone. I explained the situation to him. He said he had to make a decision in a few days, because he had to go back to France to vote at the end of the week. I raised the commitment to 95, even 97, percent. Ten days later Mechi came to New York to join me. Her first words when she got off the train were, "I've rented the house." I said, "You can't do that. What happens if we don't go abroad?" She said, "We'll move into an apartment." The next morning I was awakened in the hotel in New York by a telephone call from Washington. A feminine voice with a French accent said, "Mr. Eaton, what did you say to your wife?" I replied, sleepily, "Mrs. Marion, I said what any good husband says to his wife. 'Yes!'"

So we rented the house, and then crossed our fingers a little more tightly. The next Monday the telephone call from Personnel in Washington finally came. The voice at the other end of the line said, "It's Madrid. Ambassador Rivero has agreed."

That night we went out to dinner to celebrate and make plans for what were to be the four most fascinating—although not by any means the easiest—years of our Foreign Service experience. At one point before we actually departed for Madrid, a senior and very experienced Foreign Service officer friend said to me, "Sam, Spain sounds like a great assignment, but are you really sure it's the right thing for you if the ambassador has accepted only very reluctantly?" My reply was that, once given the opportunity, I had never had any problem convincing my bosses that I could do any Foreign Service job well. Moreover, whatever the outcome of the relationship between me and the ambassador might be, an assignment to Europe at this stage, and particularly to Spain, would be worth it.

It was.

FRANCO'S LAST TWO YEARS 1

During Franco's last years three myths prevailed at the popular level in Europe, in the United States, and indeed among many in Spain itself, that greatly blurred the general public's view of Spain. The first of these was that Franco was immortal. The second was that nothing had fundamentally changed in Spain, in the Spanish society, or in the Spanish character since the Civil War—since Hemingway, as it were—which was the last time the world had really focused its attention on Spain. The third was that Spain was a sleepy place, where very little of political, economic, or social significance had happened for decades, or would happen in the foreseeable future, and certainly not during the summer months, when everyone went off to Torremolinos.

Spain and the rest of the world had gotten very used to Franco after almost forty years of absolute power. His health was failing, and also his voice, but he seemed still to be the last word on every issue of importance in Spain and many not so important. Even when he didn't speak or act, officials and the populace thought first of what he would have said or done before they made a move—such was the force of habit and the continuing extent of his influence. In these circumstances, although it was known objectively that he was aged and infirm, and politicians and others talked about and to some extent prepared for the transition, there was an unconscious, lingering popular suspicion that he might never really die. There was, on the whole, a moratorium on major political activity, in part because living conditions in Spain at this stage of the Franco regime were so good relative to past expectations. Therefore, the talk of transition was not all that specific, the preparations were not all that concrete, and the stories of his immortality were many.*

What sort of man was it that, ill and infirm at age 82, could still so hold an already changed and vital nation in the palm of his hand and make it do his bidding? That he was a man of ability, of personal courage and of unbending will was doubted by no one. He had demonstrated this as Spain's youngest general in campaigns in Africa and Spain and as its political leader for decades. That he was an ascetic, religious, almost messianic, personally incorruptible man who was dedicated to serve Spain and God as he saw best, also no one doubted. That he despised popular politics was well known. That among his bêtes noires were political parties, Masons, and Communists was also common knowledge. Not so well understood was the degree to which he seemed to have personally favored and supported social advances for his people—the broad social security system, the low-cost housing, the expanded educational opportunities. But how did he maintain control and lead? He did it with a style and with tactics that were in sharp contrast to the popular image abroad of the Spaniard, but were quite familiar to those who knew the natives of Galicia, Franco's home region.

The "Gallegos" are the Vermonters of Spain. Their words are sparse. They turn aside questions with questions. They are hard and suspicious. They have few close friends. They are patient; they will not be hurried; they take the long view. They are not urbane, but they will never be beaten in a horse trade. There is a story of a traveler who went to Galicia and became lost on a back road. He was on vacation and in no particular hurry, but he asked a lone Gallego farmer walking down the road where the road led. The Gallegan responded by asking where he wanted to go. The traveler answered that he had no particular destination in mind. The Gallegan asked, "Then, why do you want to know?" and went on his way.

A true story was told me about Franco by a Spaniard who had known him well. One of Franco's ministers became convinced that a new policy must be adopted in his field. The minister knew Franco wouldn't like his idea, but he was certain he was right. He therefore worked for several months developing his case for the new policy, while saying nothing about it to Franco. Then, when it was all ready and carefully written up, he raised it

---

*One day in the year 2000 a large multitude of Franco's faithful followers gathered outside Franco's residence, the Pardo Palace, where Franco had fallen deathly ill, to pay homage to him and to wish him a tearful farewell. They made impassioned pleas for him to come to the balcony if his ebbing strength would permit so they might have one last sight of him alive before he went to his reward in heaven. His oldest and most trusted aide went to him filled with emotion at this demonstration of devotion and said, "Generalissimo, ten thousand of your followers have come to say goodbye to you and are waiting outside in the hope that they may see you, if only for a moment." Franco looked at his aide from his bed and said in his low, squeaky, almost inaudible voice, "Oh, where are they going?"

with Franco in one of his weekly audiences with him. Franco listened without saying a word to his impassioned thirty-minute presentation, took from him the carefully written document he proffered at the end, put it in a drawer of his desk, and then said simply, "Is that all?" The proposal was never discussed again between the two of them and, needless to say, was not acted upon.

Franco's ability to listen while his countrymen talked, to wait for the time to make a decision, and to say the absolute minimum needed—thus insuring that his every word would be listened to the more carefully—were probably important factors in his ability to lead. There doubtless were other factors. One of these was that he never let any one minister in his many governments achieve a position of great prominence. As soon as a minister became too visible and too potentially powerful on his own, he was out.

Similarly, Franco maintained a structure that assured there would always be divisions within the military, and that no single undisputed top military leader developed below him. This was why he opposed the creation of a ministry of defense, which might be led by a dangerously strong man. On this issue General Manuel Díez Alegría, chief of the High General Staff, differed with him, which was one reason he was dismissed. Moreover, Franco insisted that the military stay out of politics. It was a matter of both principle and self-protection. The military's primary role was to defend the unity and integrity of a Spain fashioned politically and socially according to the pattern Franco set. His aides in setting that pattern were mainly civilians, and they were changed periodically. An exception was Admiral Carrero Blanco, but he came late in the game when Franco was trying to prepare for continuity of policy after he was gone.

THE NEW SPAIN

While Franco's ultimate authority in his final years remained uncontested, and while the Spanish populace found it difficult really to imagine how Spain might be without him, Spain had, in fact, changed dramatically under him (although not necessarily because of him), particularly in the last fifteen years of his rule. One writer on Spain divides the Franco years into three periods: (1) the immediate post–Civil War years (1939–53), when repression and control were severe, tens of thousands were imprisoned, and poverty and malnutrition were general; (2) Spain's emergence from isolation (1953–59), when contacts grew with other countries, beginning with the United States, financial and technical assistance were provided, and modest economic growth began; (3) the transformation of the country (1959–75), as the result of dynamic economic growth beginning with the 1959 stabilization program, itself the product of ideas deriving from the contacts and training of the previous period.* In the process of this transformation, foundation stones were laid for a peaceful and successful political transition after Franco's death.

The remarkable economic boom of the 1960s was the fundamental source of change. It raised Spain's per capita income from $1,160 at the beginning of the decade to $2,841 in 1975, and its benefits reached all levels of the society. Real wages advanced at a rate of over 6 percent per year. Those surplus rural workers who did not find jobs in the burgeoning cities emigrated to other European countries with equally buoyant rates of economic growth. Unemployment in Spain declined to below 2 percent in the early 1970s. While in 1960 only 4 in every 100 families owned refrigerators, television sets and cars, now nearly 90 percent owned the basic modern appliances and every third family had a car. Moreover, educational opportunities and enrollments expanded constantly and most of the growing industrial laboring class was covered by a modern social insurance program that included health care, unemployment and disability compensation, and retirement pensions. There was an extensive low-cost housing program. There was agricultural reform in terms of improved access to land, expanded irrigation, the provision of farm machinery pools and extension service, and easier credit. The literacy rate reached 97 percent for urban families and 86 percent for farm families. All at once the Spanish common man who had been so used to poverty and hardship—and so embittered by life's material inequalities, injustices, and uncertainties—could hope for not just a bicycle, but a small car, a television set, an apartment or land of his own, education for his children, and reasonable security for himself and his family. Spain's cities grew and bustled. The percentage of the working population engaged in agriculture went from 42 in 1960 to 29 in 1970, with corresponding changes in the percentages engaged in industry and services. Spain's countryside and small towns became easier places in which to live, even though economically they did not advance as fast as the cities. Spain—and Europe—offered more alternatives, more hope, for the individual Spaniard.

The effects of the economic boom were dramatically illustrated by changes in the lives of our servants. Juan Vergara, the doorman, came from a small farming village outside Madrid. He was a child visiting relatives in Madrid when the Civil War began. He barely survived the three years of the war by living off scraps. Afterwards he returned to eke out a meager existence with his parents on the small family farm. Now in Madrid he was living comfortably and his daughters were going to excellent schools.

---

*Constantine Christopher Menges, *Spain: The Struggle for Democracy Today,* The Washington Papers, vol. 2, no. 58 (Beverly Hills and London: Sage Publications, 1978), p. 12.

Valentin Sánchez, the driver, had grown up in Madrid and suffered similar privation. He was a highly intelligent and very serious and responsible man, but his educational opportunities had been limited. Nevertheless, he now owned his own apartment and his own small car. His oldest daughter, moreover, had completed secondary school and was continuing the study of languages in college.

Mariana Ruíz, the cook, had spent the first years of her life on a farm in Andalucía. She told us that her greatest ambition as a little girl had been to have her own schoolbook. She went to school for a year or two, but her parents could not afford a book for her. She dropped out and in her early teens went to Madrid to look for work. Starting as a scullery maid, she eventually learned to cook. By the time she came to work for us, when she was in her mid-thirties, she had accumulated enough savings to make a down payment on a $25,000 apartment.

The economic boom was, in fact, transforming Spain into one of the ten or so leading industrial nations of the world. No longer, by 1970, was Spain a poor, agricultural nation. Sharp differences of income persisted, but extremes of poverty were greatly reduced. Instead, Spain was now a growing, dynamic, industrializing, modernizing, relatively affluent nation. It was modernizing, economically and socially at least, if not yet politically. And what happened economically and socially could not but affect what was to happen politically.

What produced Spain's economic boom of the 1960s? The necessary ideas came through contact with economists and technicians from the United States, from international financial agencies, and from Europe after Spain's emergence from isolation in the 1960s. The necessary institutional and policy framework came through the entrance into the Spanish government in 1957 of a group of able technocrats who presided over a basic change in Spain's economic policies, from autarchy and controls to openness, deregulation, and reliance on competition and market forces. The stabilization program they instituted in 1959 was a textbook success. Its long-term results should be studied by those who question the political and social as well as economic importance and potential of such programs.

At the same time, prosperity in the rest of Europe provided stimulating markets, a needed demand for surplus Spanish labor, and a windfall of tourists—hordes of tourists from the north looking for the sun. In 1960 the total number of tourists per annum had reached the level of Spain's population, thirty-five million. By 1978 it had reached forty million. These tourists, primarily from Europe but also from the United States and many other countries, brought with them not only economically invigorating infusions of foreign exchange but also customs, ideas, and examples that were bound to affect and influence Spanish mores.

The Idea of Democracy. Among the ideas they carried with them was the idea of democracy. Not that this was a new concept. Most Europeans had been expressing their own dedication to democracy by example, word, and deed for centuries, and their concern over authoritatianism in Spain by word and deed for decades. Nor were the tourists, by what they did and said and how they acted, the main and most important purveyors of the democratic idea. It was simply that they added to its currency in thousands of ways and through millions of contacts.

What kind of democracy? Because of the geographical proximity of the rest of Europe and historical links with it, parliamentary democracy was naturally the type the Spaniards came to think about—with or without a constitutional monarchy and, for many, with a moderate socialist, welfare-state bias. Not that the Spaniards thought in any detail in this period about the organizations and procedures—the institutions—such a democracy would require. But certainly they thought considerably about the lifeblood of this type of democracy—freedom of expression, of assembly, and of association—for that was where existing restraints most clearly limited them.

THE IMPETUS FOR CHANGE

Thus a quite remarkable sense of well-being, except for the nagging and growing desire for greater political liberties, pervaded most of Spain in the last years of Franco. The material standard of living had improved beyond all expectations of most of the population. Political repression was at a low level and now affected directly only a few. The public order situation was in hand except for the occasional terrorist act; the ordinary citizen could be more confident of his personal physical security than in most countries of the world. There was a habit of self-discipline ingrained by past experience, coupled with considerable scope for Spanish individuality. Indicative of the relative lack of tension and conflict in the society was the remarkably low level of its prison population. Only some ten thousand Spaniards out of a population of thirty-five million were in prison in 1975 and about half of these were political prisoners. Comparable figures for the United States in that year were two hundred forty-one thousand out of a population of two hundred twenty million—a proportion of about one to one thousand in contrast to one to thirty-five hundred in the Spanish case. This sense of well-being and indeed of relaxation led Aleksandr Solzhenitsyn to make a remark during a visit to Spain that was quite exasperating to many Spaniards who remembered especially the degree of political repression during the early Franco years. He said, in effect, "You Spaniards have no idea what a dictatorship can be like."

The general well-being, although still marred by lack of freedom of political expression and participation, was no negligible achievement. Those Spaniards who remembered or thought about the poverty and chaos of the early 1930s or the subsequent Civil War tended to be chary of radical change. They were all the more concerned, then, as to whether Spain could indeed handle itself without severe disruption and violence after Franco passed from the scene. At the same time, Franco was in fact aging and making his own preparations for the ultimate transition, even though the populace, accustomed to his complete control, did not give those preparations the importance that, in retrospect, was their due. His most decisive act was to determine that the monarchy should be restored after his death and to name Prince Juan Carlos de Borbón, himself a young man born after the end of the Civil War, as his ultimate successor as chief of state. One of the greatest political problems faced by dictators is how to arrange satisfactorily for their own succession. Franco did this with unusual foresight, although one may rightly wonder whether he would agree, were he to return now to earth, that he had done so successfully, that is, had arranged that policies dear to him would be continued.* Franco believed in the idea of a monarchy. He saw the need for an institutional link between the past and the future, a link to be established before his death. He himself ruled like a monarch—an ascetic, conservative monarch to be sure, but a powerful one who set store by the symbols, protocol, and ceremony of power, though he stopped short of identifying himself as royalty. He rejected Juan Carlos's father, Don Juan, as his successor as chief of state because Don Juan was too liberal, too democratic. He doubtless hoped, and expected, to be able to train young Juan Carlos to continue his own policies. Franco also furthered the preparations for transition when, in July 1973, he gave up the day-to-day duties of head of government and arranged for the naming of his trusted friend and colleague, Admiral Luis Carrero Blanco, as his prime minister. True, Carrero Blanco was handpicked to carry on the Francoist tradition whether or not Franco was there, but the simple act of delegating the prime ministership was an important institutional change for the future.

Impetus for a somewhat accelerated movement toward political change came from an unexpected source in December 1973. A bold group of terrorists presumed to be from the extreme Basque nationalist group, ETA (Basque Homeland and Freedom), assassinated Carrero Blanco. Suddenly Franco was faced with the need to find a new prime minister, and—also suddenly—even regime political figures were shocked into thinking a bit more urgently about mortality and the need for preparing the transition.

---

*This latter point is made trenchantly and hilariously in a Spanish bestseller of 1978 entitled *And After Three Years He Rose From the Dead,* by Fernando Vizcaino Casas.

The Spirit of February 12. The new prime minister named by Franco turned out to be Carlos Arias Navarro, a former director general of security (i.e., head of the national police), later a respected mayor of Madrid, and then minister of government. Probably he was named in part because of his police experience. If so, his primary policy emphasis, as it turned out, was a surprise. On February 12, 1974, he made a major policy speech that signaled his intention to proceed with the gradual opening up of the Spanish political system. The speech was cautiously drafted and would scarcely have seemed to anyone to set forth an ambitious program except to those who had lived under forty years of authoritarianism. To them and to Spain it did. It called for the passage by the usually obedient Cortes (the Spanish legislature) of three laws for political change. One was to authorize and set the conditions for "political associations" (the term "political parties" was an absolute no-no in Francoland); a second was to provide for the popular election of mayors and other municipal officials; and a third was to prohibit certain senior government officials (undersecretaries, assistant secretaries, and the like) from being members of the legislature while holding their high-level government positions. Arias not only called for these laws; he also set a timetable for their passage, and talked of the need to begin the accommodation to "change from a system of adhesion to one person to a system of popular participation through institutions." Meanwhile, an Arias appointee as minister of information and culture, Pio Cabanillas, was following surprisingly liberal press and media policies. Things were being written and said publicly that would not have been permitted in previous years. There was proliferation of new magazines concentrating on political reporting and commentary. Political discussion groups began to surface. One man who had previously made a reputation as an organizer of hunts where the ambitious could meet ministers and even, perhaps, Franco, now significantly turned to organizing Madrid's most prestigious political discussion group, where aspiring politicians coveted the opportunity to speak. The new, more liberal atmosphere was dubbed the Spirit of February 12. There was an air of expectation as to what might happen politically.

This air quickened almost palpably when, on July 9, 1974, Franco entered the hospital with phlebitis—thus ending, for some years to come at least, the myth that nothing happens in Spain in the summer. Weeks of uncertainty and ambiguity followed. Prince Juan Carlos was called urgently to the hospital and made acting chief of state. But what did this mean? Did it mean that Franco would not return, and that Juan Carlos could now begin to lead as he would wish? Most certainly not, at least in the latter regard. Franco's entrenched disciples would see to that for the foreseeable future, so long as Franco was alive and coherent, even were Franco to retire to his beloved Galicia. What, in any event, were Juan Carlos' desires? Not many people knew. His public image was that of a handsome, not very communicative young man who loved sports, who lived constantly in Franco's shadow, and who was most often characterized as "prudent." Privately, as the American Embassy knew, he was impatient for the time when he would take over and concerned over the ambiguity of a situation in which he was formally acting chief of state but in reality had very little room for maneuver and action. Moreover, he was apprehensive lest circumstances during his time as acting chief of state create situations in which he might have to do things that would jeopardize his future stewardship.

The days passed into weeks. Franco continued in the hospital and speculation increased that he would not return but rather would retire to Galicia. Such was the betting among many in the diplomatic corps, but the US ambassador, retired Admiral Horacio Rivero, did not agree. Ambassador Rivero was a shrewd, astute man, who, as he said, had made a careful study of Franco, and believed he understood him. Rivero was convinced that Franco would not give up power until he was either dead or totally incapable. Rivero surprised his diplomatic colleagues by predicting flatly that Franco would return. And he was entirely right.

Franco Returns. After Franco had been in the hospital several weeks and had spent a further twenty-four days vacationing and recuperating in Galicia, Spain awakened to the news one morning that he had resumed his functions as chief of state and that Prince Juan Carlos had returned to the wings from his brief period on center stage. Franco returned not only formally and physically but also, as was soon to be apparent, spiritually. It became clear over the next weeks that he was not at all comfortable with the Spirit of February 12 and that he would not let it get out of hand. Two events had already given warning of this: a strong speech in April by a still very influential ex-minister and champion of right conservatism, José Antonio Girón; and the sacking in June of the liberal-minded chief of the High General Staff of the armed forces, General Manuel Díez Alegría. Now in October, after Franco's return, came the sudden firing of Minister of Culture and Information Pio Cabanillas, whose more open media policy did not please the Right. One story had it that Girón had carefully built up a dossier on Cabanillas that included examples of stories being printed in the press and magazines, ranging from ones that, to the minds of the puritanically minded Francoists, were indecent, to ones that intimated corruption on the part of members of the Franco family. With Cabanillas went, in sympathy, his undersecretary Marcelino Oreja, later to be foreign minister under the King; First Vice-President and Minister of Finance Antonio Barrera Irimo; and the head of the National Institute for Industry, Francisco Fernández Ordóñez, an intimate of Barrera's who was later to be minister of finance in the King's second government. The road for the three modest political measures called for in Arias's speech of February 12 now became more difficult, and the measures were watered down.

Some predicted that Arias would soon have to leave office because of his differences with Franco. But Franco was loath to change prime ministers too often. Arias was only the second delegated one he had had; to bring in a new one after just a year could be interpreted as a sign of weakness. To the credit of Arias, he persisted in his efforts at liberalization despite Franco's misgivings. He made sure that the legislation on political associations passed the Cortes by the end of 1974 as he had promised, even if in a watered-down version; and during 1975 political associations began to form. The other two legs of his reform effort—provision for election of municipal officials and for banning simultaneous tenure in certain high executive offices and in the legislature—continued under consideration. There were reports of continuing differences between Franco and Arias with a corresponding enhancement of Arias's image as a true, though modest, reformer battling against odds.

Most of 1975 was a story of tugging and hauling between those who wished to move modestly forward on the political front and those who wished to hold back the clock; there were also rumors of deterioration in Franco's health countered by stories and symbols of his continued vitality. Political associations were formed, but none that would be any threat to the regime. One major political figure, Manuel Fraga Iribarne, tested the waters in February and drew back. There were reports of some political unrest at the lower levels of the armed forces, and the government responded at the end of July by arresting nine members of a shadowy Military Democratic Union—eight captains and one major. These middle-grade officers appeared to be interested in both political and professional reforms, but not to have gone much beyond the stage of discussion groups or to have gathered much of a following yet. Terrorist activity was increasing in the Basque country and elsewhere; some forty killings were attributed to terrorists over a two-year period. The government responded on September 27, 1975, with the execution of five terrorists convicted by military courts of material involvement in the killing of police. The executions were widely disapproved in the rest of Europe as evidence of continued repressiveness within Spain.

In the latter months of 1974 and throughout 1975, the top political leaders sensed that Franco probably was indeed a very ill man and could not live much longer. Accordingly, they talked more than in the past of transition arrangements. In early October 1975 at lunch in my home Adolfo Suárez, then the young head of the principal political association, which was government-sponsored, argued that it was time for Franco to resign in favor of Juan Carlos. This was a surprisingly bold stand for a man in his position to be taking. It presaged his later position to an extent we could not know at the time.

Meanwhile the regime's public relations apparatus, and Franco himself, did their best to give the impression that he was in fine shape. The media showed pictures and told stories of his playing golf every afternoon during the summer. Franco appeared at military parades just as he had always done, and stood for long periods of time returning the salutes of the passing troops. When President Ford visited Spain in May, Franco met all his obligations in a full schedule; he even insisted on taking the president to the airport for an early morning departure after a very busy day and evening. In their conversation over coffee before going to the airport they talked of golf and hunting; Franco demonstrated his techniques and insisted that he was still in fine fettle for these sports. Those of us who worked on the preparations for President Ford's visit knew, however, how much care had to be taken over such details as how Franco was to get in and out of his limousine, and how unusual it was for him to be so active at eight o'clock in the morning.

End of an Era. In mid-October 1975 Franco was reported ill again. This was at first denied, and on October 19 he presided over a cabinet meeting. Immediately thereafter he entered the hospital. There followed a month of agonizing deterioration in his health; although all possible medical efforts to keep him alive were employed, he was proved mortal. He died on November 20, 1975. Spain was a scene of disbelief and mourning. Long, solemn, sad lines formed to pass his coffin. Prime Minister Arias read Franco's last political testament over television with a voice choked with emotion and tears in his eyes. Sympathy had been aroused by the minutely reported details of his stubborn battle against death. His memory was respected by many. At the same time, many—subsequent voting indicated most—others were relieved; and in a number of homes there were irreverent openings of champagne. His memory and references to him passed surprisingly quickly into the background for most after his death.

Thus on Franco's death Spain was divided in its view of this singular leader, who had controlled the nation for forty years. The degree of division, and the balance of political forces, were to be seen much more clearly over the months that ensued, particularly in the results of the elections held for the first time nineteen months later. For US relations with Spain, it was essential that the balance of political forces be judged accurately. Contacts with the prospective new leadership had to be cultivated even while the old leadership was still in place.

THE **UNITED STATES** BETWEEN **PAST** AND **FUTURE** *2*

A very touchy problem dominated US relations with Spain during the last year's of Franco's life. On the one hand, the United States had a strong interest in continuing an effective security relationship with the Franco regime. On the other hand, it was also important to prepare the way for productive relations with whatever regime or regimes came after Franco. The question was how could these two often conflicting objectives be accomplished together.

THE MILITARY AGREEMENT OF 1953

For over twenty years, since 1953, the United States had had a military agreement with Spain under which American military forces had the use of extensive facilities at Spanish air and naval bases while their Spanish counterparts were provided with various types of American training and assistance. The decision to seek and enter into such an agreement in the early 1950s represented for the United States the placing of military security considerations above considerations of political principle. This, of course, was not the first time in our history that we had done so (witness our wartime relationship with Stalin, for instance), nor would it be the last. A nation will always—or almost always—place matters of survival before political ideals, given that stark choice to make. The problem of decision making in such cases is not really so much one of the principle involved as it is one of estimating the true strength of the survival argument (admittedly, the degree to which particular decision makers are devoted to particular political ideals is also a factor). Alternatives are seldom stark, and decisions are always subjective. The decision with regard to Spain in 1953 was a controversial one, made at a time when security issues ranked high in the minds of our government leaders and our nation, and when our president was a military man.

Spain, for its part, was also divided about the 1953 agreement with the United States. But in Spain at that time the debate turned more on political than on military considerations, as it has continued to do ever since. It is important to understand this fundamental difference of perspective, because it explains much about the negotiation and functioning of successive agreements over the years.

For Franco, whose voice was the only one that counted in Spain in 1953, the agreement was a breakthrough that would help move Spain out of the international isolation it had experienced since the defeat of the Axis Powers. Whether, as is argued by many, this was particularly beneficial to Franco in terms of his own position in Spain, is open to question. Franco, like many other leaders at other times in other countries, had reaped very considerable internal benefits simply by standing up to foreign affronts. At the same time, however, he took great satisfaction in the breakup of the major allies' common political front against Spain. Moreover—but I believe secondarily in Franco's mind—the agreement with the United States was attractive because it would bring with it considerable economic and military assistance.

To the political opposition groups in Spain the agreement was anathema for a variety of reasons whose applicability for each group depended upon where the group was in the political spectrum. The far Right didn't like it because it implied undue dependence on and a potentially contaminating association with a soft, overly liberal democracy. The Communists didn't like it because it moved Spain more firmly and actively into the camp of the anticommunist powers in the cold war. The Socialists and other anti-Franco groups, including the Basques, who together in the end were to be proven more numerous and more influential than the far Right or the Communists, didn't like it primarily because they saw it as supporting Franco and the type of regime he represented. I personally would argue, and have argued, that they were quite wrong in this assessment. Franco was well entrenched in Spain at the time of the agreement and there was no imminent prospect of his removal. The only circumstances that might have led to his earlier departure, I believe, would have been assassination or a breakdown of the system over which he ruled. Neither of these circumstances was in the cards. In that situation, the best hope for the end of authoritarianism, the return of democracy, and the opportunity for anti-Franco political groups to participate and compete in the political process was economic and social progress. Only thus would there be a reduction in the social tensions that had contributed to such severe conflict, and to the regression to authoritarianism. The agreement with the United States and the process it encouraged supported that economic and social progress, and thus the ultimate return of Spain to democracy, much more, I am convinced, than it supported Franco and Francoism. True, the agreement made Franco's rule easier; but not decisively so. This is an important judgment to which we will return later in another context.

For Western Europeans the agreement was cause for a severe case of political schizophrenia. On the one hand, such close association with Franco went against their democratic principles at least in the short term, which is the time span on which politicians in democracies naturally concentrate. On the other hand, it contributed to their security, and thus incidentally to the security of their democracies. In cold fact, their situation was ideal: they could have their cake and eat it too. They could remain politically aloof from Franco's Spain while at the same time Spain became a de facto partner in the NATO security network. In fact, too, their political stance was in its way helpful to the eventual democratization effort in Spain. By maintaining their aloofness they continually underlined to the Spanish populace the importance of democratic principles, while conveniently doing nothing to stem the increased flow of trade, investment, and tourism that accompanied the opening up and economic and social progress of Spain that was to be so helpful, in due course, to the political liberalization effort. Thus there was an unusually felicitous complementarity to the different political stances toward Spain adopted by the United States and by Europe.

The agreement of 1953 had established the underlying principles. At roughly five-year intervals thereafter, US and Spanish negotiators concentrated on the secondary though important issues of how much and what kind of military and economic assistance to offer in exchange for what use of Spanish military facilities by US forces. The length, detail and—at times— suspense of these negotiations belied the fact that the negotiators were always destined to eventual agreement because: (1) for the United States, the security argument in favor of agreement continued strong enough to induce compromise at reasonable, but not really very high, levels of military and economic assistance; (2) for Spain, the political convenience and mutual security interest of agreement were enough to induce acceptance of military and economic aid at levels considerably below the original asking price, even though the United States could not deliver on Spain's principal objective of full political acceptance in the Atlantic community. In the end, Franco would always tell his negotiators to accept. This he quite evidently did once again before his death in 1975, although the final details of the agreement then being negotiated were not actually completed until after his death. When the agreement was finally signed, shortly after Juan Carlos became King, the mix of reasons for both the US and the Spanish interest in agreement had been significantly changed because of the change in Spanish leadership. In the US case, indeed, the case for agreement was more compelling than before Franco's death, while being at least as compelling for the new Spanish regime.

THE 1974–76 NEGOTIATIONS

The initial position of the Spanish representatives in the negotiation that began in 1974 and was finally completed in February 1976 included the following three principal points.

(1) *Spain should receive a specific security guarantee, either in its bilateral agreement with the United States or by becoming a member of NATO.* The argument Spanish negotiators made for this point was that Spain had placed itself at great risk: it had committed itself to the Western defense system to the extent of permitting foreign troops to be based on its soil and thus of inviting direct involvement in any eventual major conflict. This argument made a certain amount of sense from the Spanish perspective, which deemphasized security considerations and emphasized political ones. The unstated and more compelling corollary was that a specific security guarantee from the United States or, better, acceptance into NATO would be a major step toward the achievement of the fuller international political acceptability that the Franco regime so much wanted.

From the United States perspective, the central Spanish argument for a security guarantee was not a strong one because the United States assumed that Spain had the same basic security interests as did it; that the bilateral agreement with the United States enhanced Spanish security because it materially supported the NATO deterrent to Warsaw Pact aggression; that were there to be a war Spain would be targeted by the Soviet Union in one way or another, sooner or later; and that the existing arrangements tied Spain, the United States, and Europe together as fully and effectively as would any formal security guarantee. Moreover, there was no practical possibility of achieving either Senate agreement to a formal security guarantee for Spain or NATO acceptance of Spain so long as Franco ruled.

(2) *The US military presence in Spain should be reduced substantially.* The main focus in this regard was on the nuclear presence, in part because of the 1966 Palomares incident, when four nuclear bombs were accidentally dropped on Spanish territory (but did not detonate). Also at issue was the use of Spanish bases by US air-refueling tankers, in part because of Spanish suspicion that such tankers had been used to refuel planes going to the Middle East during the Yom Kippur war. If they had, the US action would not only have gone beyond the scope of the agreement for the use of Spanish base facilities but would also have damaged traditional Spanish efforts to maintain good relations with the Arab countries.

(3) *United States military assistance to Spain should be higher.* A great
deal of rhetoric was devoted to this point by the Spanish side, but it was
noteworthy that the Spanish military experts were unprepared until late in
the negotiations to offer specifics about the type and amounts of equipment they wanted. Moreover, their minds changed in this regard even
after the negotiations had ended. The truth of the matter was that the
Spanish military during this period had no clear concept of its mission,
and no strong central authority short of Franco. Thus it had no coherent
and agreed internal position on its need for equipment. Not that this
mattered all that much. From the Spanish point of view, at least (as we
have seen) at the top, the principal objective of the agreements was
political, not military. And from the US point of view the principal objective was use of Spanish base facilities. Strengthening and further modernizing the Spanish military forces was, for both sides, a desirable but
secondary objective.

The initial position of the United States negotiators comprised three
principal points:

(1) *There could be no security guarantee.* The reason was that guarantee
could not (for the reasons above outlined) gain approval, either bilaterally,
from the US Senate, or multilaterally, through NATO membership. There
could, however, be general statements of principle that would help with
public relations and express in language that was not legally binding, what
was in any event a de facto security relationship. (Such statements of
principle were developed and agreed to.)

(2) *The United States should be permitted to retain all existing base facility
privileges.* In practice, this meant all the facilities that it had at the outset
of the negotiations. (This position modified as the negotiations progressed.)

(3) *The United States was prepared to provide modest but broadly based
assistance.* In other words, it would provide not only military assistance
but continuing and perhaps expanded assistance for scientific, technological, and educational exchanges. It was also prepared to consult more
closely and effectively on economic issues. (This position did not change
substantially during the negotiations.)

The role played by the United States Embassy provides an interesting
sidelight on the preparation of the US position and the actual conduct of the
negotiations. During the initial stage of preparations for negotiation, Admiral
Rivero was still US ambassador to Spain. He had already reached his own
conclusions on the logical eventual outcome of the negotiations, and had
freely stated them to the Joint Chiefs of Staff—where as a former deputy
chief of naval operations he easily obtained a hearing—and to others in
Washington. However, what he had to say was not entirely to the liking of
the authorities in Washington, particularly the military ones.

The Astilleros Españoles Company builds a variety of ships at its San Carlos Shipyard in Cadiz. During Franco's later years Spanish industry surged ahead, encouraging the forces of modernization—and democratization.

Franco (back to camera) during the last year of his life: at this credentials presentation ceremony he is shaking hands with the chief of the US Military Mission to Spain, Admiral William Lemos. Other participants: Foreign Minister Pedro Cortina (left, in full Spanish diplomatic uniform); newly arrived American Ambassador Wells Stabler (immediately to Franco's right); and the author (to the right of Stabler).

Diplomacy informal—and formal. *Above*: Mechi (the author's wife) and an admirer before the 17th-century Spanish tapestry that hangs at the head of the stairs to the main reception area at Don Ramón de la Cruz 3, the Eatons' home in Madrid. *Below*: One of the twice-yearly meetings of the Spanish-American Council under the Treaty of Friendship and Cooperation. Seated (from left to right): Ambassador Wells Stabler; Secretary of State Cyrus Vance; General George S. Brown, chairman of the Joint Chiefs of Staff; Assistant Secretary Arthur Hartman; and the author. (Picture taken May 11, 1977, in the Ambassadors' Room of the Santa Cruz Palace, that is, the Foreign Ministry in Madrid.)

Spain after Franco's death became more active diplomatically. *Above*: King Juan Carlos and Queen Sofía being received at Barajas Airport, Madrid, by the author and his wife upon the King's return from the United States in May 1976. *Below*: Prime Minister Adolfo Suárez (civilian clothes, right) being greeted, upon his return from a visit to the United States, by First Vice-President for Defense Affairs Gutiérrez Mellado. Descending the stairs: Foreign Minister Marcelino Oreja. (Picture taken at Barajas Airport, April 30, 1977.)

The first Basque parliament under the 1978 Constitution stands before the famous Tree of Guernica, symbol of Basque nationalism for over a century, while being addressed by Carlos Garaicoechea, president of the Basque Regional Government (left, at microphone). The temple-like building is the old Casa de Juntas, traditional meeting place for heads of Basque townships.

The mayor of Oñate, a center of Basque culture close to Bilbao, makes a point to the author with characteristic Basque vehemence during one of the author's periodic visits to that region. Also present: a priest (rector of the University of Oñate) and two town councillors. (Picture taken in 1977.)

I had just arrived in Madrid from the State Department Planning and Coordination Staff. It was natural for me to want to see a series of basic studies done on the issues likely to arise in the negotiations. Since Washington did not seem inclined to undertake the studies at that time—probably because it wanted to avoid possible bureaucratic confrontations at this stage—I, with Ambassador Rivero's encouragement, formed and chaired a task force of the Country Team in Madrid to produce them. This, too, made Washington (particularly the military) uncomfortable, the more so when our task force came to much the same conclusions as had Ambassador Rivero (who was, after all, a retired admiral). Later I learned, somewhat to my pain, the extent and reach of Washington's discomfort when a Foreign Service inspector, acting upon a complaint from some military officials in Washington, raised with me in all seriousness the propriety of Embassy Madrid's having undertaken these studies. Obviously, his views of an embassy's appropriate role did not agree with mine. I gained some small satisfaction later when the final US position near the end of the negotiations—although not the final results of the negotiations—very nearly paralleled the recommendations the embassy's task force had produced at the beginning.

The Conduct of the Negotiations. An ambassador is the president's personal representative abroad. His business is not just the business of the State Department but that of all government agencies having interests in the country to which he is assigned.

Presidents since Kennedy have written circular letters to their ambassadors making clear to them and to all government personnel concerned that the ambassador is in charge of all US government activities in the country to which he is accredited—all, that is, except those under certain military commands and some aspects of CIA functions. The good ambassador takes this broad responsibility seriously and spends much time making sure the activities of all US government agencies under his care make sense, and are properly coordinated and consistent with US policy and interests in that country. In carrying out this coordinating and policy function, he will often call for assistance on the career Foreign Service personnel working under him. In particular, he will turn to his deputy chief of mission, who is normally looked upon as his alter ego. Thus it was not strange that I, with the agreement of the ambassador, should have undertaken studies on a military issue that had political overtones.

This seems very neat organizationally, but there are two problems. First, other agencies do not always readily accept ambassadorial leadership, and, as has been noted, certain military commands are excluded from the ambassador's purview. Second, in Washington final coordination is only achieved at the level of the president. Unless the president clearly delegates coordinating functions, the various departments and agencies naturally tend to maintain their independence of position until an issue reaches him.

Aside from preparation of positions, much depends, in any negotiations, on the principal negotiators. In this case, the negotiating teams were led by two able, low-key, patient diplomats: Undersecretary of Foreign Affairs Juan José Rovira for Spain, and Ambassador Robert McCloskey for the United States. The negotiations moved at a stately pace for a year; the teams met roughly once a month, alternating between Madrid and Washington. Members of the two teams got to know each other well. They liked each other. A certain camaraderie developed, and neither side seemed in a great hurry. At the end of a year considerable progress had been made, but agreement had not yet been reached. The September 1975 termination date of the current agreement was approaching. Therefore an extension was required and quickly agreed to. At this point, Spanish Foreign Minister Pedro Cortina Mauri involved himself directly in the negotiations; he was probably acting under Franco's specific instructions. In meetings with Secretary of State Henry Kissinger in Washington, Cortina reached a framework agreement that brought the negotiations near to a close.

Cortina was a veteran Spanish career diplomat who was close to the Franco family and who liked to do things for himself. He was as thin as Kissinger was rotund. The pressure of being foreign secretary seemed to keep him slender, by aggravating his stomach problems, in the same way that it led Secretary Kissinger to eat more and so gain weight. Cortina was also as legalistic and pedantic in his approach as Kissinger was conceptual. Cortina was as dry as Kissinger was humorous. It would be difficult to find two more different men, except for two things. They were both highly intelligent and they both got great pleasure out of hearing themselves express their own views.

As might have been expected, Cortina sought to draft the framework agreement more in terms of language dealing philosophically with Spain's role in the West, and with the general security relationship, than he did in terms of reducing the US military presence or increasing US military assistance. In fact, he was more concessionary in attitude than we had anticipated.

Then an entirely new factor entered the negotiations. Franco died. The negotiators had proceeded with their business as though Franco's health were not a factor. They had been deliberate in pace, but not because of his health. Neither side could predict when he might die. Both sides wanted to continue the relationship whether he died or not. What changed with his death was that the United States could now go further politically than before. It could, for instance, offer a full treaty relationship, instead of another executive agreement, although it still could not provide a specific security guarantee. The Senate was not favorably disposed to new commitments of this nature in the aftermath of Vietnam, and the European NATO countries wanted to wait and see how serious Spain without Franco would be about democracy.

One of the first acts of the first government under King Juan Carlos was to make clear to the United States that it wanted to bring the negotiations to a close and sign a new agreement as quickly as possible. This was done in a meeting between Foreign Minister Areilza (who had replaced Cortina) and Secretary Kissinger in Paris in December 1975. Areilza asked for three things: a treaty, a total value of assistance to Spain of $1 billion, and language that expressed the connection between Spain's defense arrangements and Western security. He also wanted to be certain there would be a definite date for the departure of US nuclear submarines from Rota and an agreement against secret clauses. In addition, there were to be certain specific reductions in the United States presence. These points all now seemed reasonable, and the negotiators went to work to complete the details of a long and complex treaty document every word of which was to be made public upon signing. Work was completed and the treaty was signed on January 24. It was apparent that it would have no problem in the US Congress, particularly now that Franco was gone and Juan Carlos had committed Spain to democracy. It was also apparent that in Spain, although the Socialists and the Communists had expressed opposition to the agreement, their primary concentration for some time would be on internal matters; they were not prepared at this time to make an issue over the continuance of Spain's bilateral military relationship with the United States. The treaty did after all provide for "denuclearization," including the removal of the nuclear submarine squadron from Rota by 1979, and for reduction of the number of air-refueling tankers based in Spain to an upper level of five. These provisions helped make it possible for them to remain quiescent on the bases issue.

With the signing of the treaty, the first principal objective of the United States in its relationship with Spain in this period—the continuance of an effective security relationship—was achieved.

GETTING READY FOR THE NEW REGIME

The second principal objective of the United States in its relations with Spain during 1974 and 1975 was to prepare the way for productive relations with whatever regime or regimes followed Franco. This objective was served well by the new treaty, as it turned out, simply because it was signed after Franco's death instead of before, and because its completion could be portrayed as an act of support for democratization in Spain under Juan Carlos, as indeed it was. In this connection, the Senate's formal expression of its hope and intention that the treaty would help Spain's progress toward free institutions was a very positive act, and was so viewed by Spanish democrats. The expression, sponsored by Senators Clark and Eagleton, read as follows:

> (1) The United States, recognizing the aspiration of Spain to achieve full participation in the political and economic institutions of Western Europe, and recognizing further that the development of free institutions in Spain is a necessary aspect of Spain's full integration into European life, hopes and intends that this Treaty will serve to support and foster Spain's progress toward free institutions and toward Spain's participation in the institutions of Western European political and economic cooperation. . . .*

The utility of the treaty in these respects was a fortunate accident of timing rather than a consciously planned political strategy, since no one knew when Franco would die. However, it does underline in retrospect the importance of doing whatever was feasible to prepare for the future during the months prior to Franco's death.

That "whatever" came down primarily, although not exclusively, to anticipating who might be the principal leaders of the future, and to establishing as good relations as possible with them in advance. All this meant identification by embassy personnel on the scene of the most likely prospective leaders, making contact with them, developing personal relations of confidence, and arranging (through trips to the United States and through dialogue) for them to acquire a better understanding of the United States, its interests, and its policies.

There is, of course, no certain, scientific, precise way of identifying potential future leaders, especially when the task has to be performed by a relatively few people in an embassy in a relatively large country. But one can do surprisingly well by being systematic about it. The system that I organized for our embassy in Madrid was as follows. The principal members of the Embassy concerned with political, military, and economic matters first reached a consensus on the main current and prospective power centers in the Spanish society. We then carefully worked out a list of the present leaders of those power centers, of those close to present leaders, and of younger men who seemed to have particular potential. Responsibility for meeting and maintaining contact with the people on this list was divided

---

*US Senate, Committee on Foreign Relations, *Executive Report No. 25 on The Treaty of Friendship and Cooperation With Spain* (Washington, DC: May 20, 1976).

among the officers of the embassy, according to their functional specialties or their rank. The list was periodically revised. People on it were met simply by calling on them in their offices, or in the normal course of diplomatic social events.

Don Ramón de la Cruz 3. Diplomatic lunches, dinners, and receptions are a vital part of the process of getting to know a country's leaders and developing effective working relations with them. The setting for these events can be important. In Madrid, Mechi and I had the advantage of being able to carry out this part of our responsibilities in one of the most fascinating residences in the Foreign Service. Our home in Spain was at Don Ramón de la Cruz 3, in the heart of the fine Salamanca residential and shopping district in the center of Madrid. It was a jewel, we were told before going to Spain in 1974. It had been built by the Viscount of Llanteno in the latter part of the nineteenth century. Some years after its completion, the viscount courted and won a young beauty of Madrid. After he died, ten or fifteen years later, his widow—still quite young and very attractive—remained in the house, becoming a well-known figure in Madrid's society and politics. In due course, it is said, she became a great and good friend of Spain's leader at that time, Primo de Rivera, and later the first woman member of the Madrid Municipal Council. But in the 1920s she fell upon hard times and was obliged to sell her home.

The buyers were Mr. and Mrs. Arthur Byne, an American couple. He was an architect and an amateur painter. They dealt in art and antiques; he painted a bit; she wrote a bit. She did books for the Hispanic Society of America; he illustrated them with photos and sketches. William Randolph Hearst contracted with them to buy Spanish art and artifacts for San Simeon. Most important for us, they set about to create a seventeenth-century atmosphere in the mansion at Don Ramón de la Cruz 3. They installed ceilings, windows, floors, fireplaces, coats of arms, paintings, furniture, tapestries, and artifacts from all over Spain. The result was an extraordinary mixture of museum and home. Some visitors during that period said the balance was a bit too much toward museum, but no one could deny the uniqueness of their creation nor its interest.

Unfortunately, after much of the transformation had been completed, the Bynes became estranged. Arthur Byne left Spain for a time, but in the mid–1930s petitioned Mrs. Byne for agreement to his return, which was granted. He was on his way back in 1935 when he died in an automobile accident in southern Spain. Mrs. Byne continued on in Don Ramón de la Cruz 3 until her own death in 1941.

The residence was left in trust under arrangements that allowed the US government first to rent it and use it for the Office of War Information and as a cultural center, and then to buy it with all its contents of art, furniture, and tapestries for a token sum. It was occupied for a time after World War II by the US chargé and has for the past thirty years been the residence of the deputy chief of mission (or minister counselor of embassy). Thus our good fortune to live there from 1974 to 1978.

This potentially most attractive relic of the past had fallen on hard times before our arrival. It was in ill repair and many of the furnishings, paintings, and tapestries that were an integral part of its decor had been taken elsewhere. Thus, in 1974, the jewel was not as much of a treasure as we had been led to expect. But in due time most of the wandering articles were recovered. Through Mechi's ingenuity, hard work, and good taste, Don Ramón de la Cruz 3 was repaired and redecorated in such a way that a proper balance was achieved between museum and home. Through her organizational ability and flair for entertaining, social events there were always a pleasure. The receptions and dinners were normally for couples, but the many lunches with political and economic leaders or leaders-to-be did not normally include wives. However, the planning for these affairs and the direction of the staff that produced them very much involved Mechi. In recognition of this, one Spanish political leader offered a touching and most appropriate toast at lunch one day to "the lady upstairs," and later sent a book on Spain to her dedicated with these words: "To the invisible Mrs. Eaton, with great appreciation."

By no means did all of those whom the embassy identified as potential leaders achieve leadership. But many did. I take some personal pride in the fact that about one-third of the members of King Juan Carlos's first three cabinets had been to my home for lunch, dinner, or drinks before they became ministers. They included Prime Minister Suárez, three of the five vice prime ministers who have held office thus far under the King, and both of his foreign ministers to date. The embassy sought out not only prospective members of early post-Franco governments. It also got to know leaders of prospective democratic opposition groups, including the Socialists, who were certain to have an important role to play in the politics of the future. These opposition groups could play a strong blocking role regarding matters of great interest to the United States, including its security relationship with Spain. Moreover, as it turned out, the Socialists became a realistic alternative to the Spanish political center as the governing force in Spain.

Problems of a Diplomat. The air of political expectation that prevailed in Spain in 1974 and 1975, with the vitality—and, normally, the responsiveness—of those with whom we made contact, lent a special flavor to this part of our job. There could be problems, however. The Franco regime was, of course, sensitive to the extent and level of our contacts with its opposition, and not everyone in our own government felt we should be seeing as wide a range of people as we were. An anecdote will illustrate the type of problem we faced with both governments.

In December 1975, our embassy in Madrid arranged a lunch with some members of the political opposition for a mid-level official of the Department of State who was passing through. The guests were people whom members of the embassy staff saw from time to time without repercussion. What tweaked the Spanish government's sensitivities on this occasion was that these people were being seen by a fairly high-level official from Washington. After this lunch a Spanish Foreign Office official complained bitterly to an old American friend of his, a Pentagon member of our negotiating team who was in town at the time, and who had had considerable experience with the political protocol of Madrid in earlier years. Subsequently the same Foreign Office official complained to me. I was chargé d'affaires at the time and suggested that we discuss the matter over lunch. At our lunch the following week, I heard him out. He had had time to get instructions from higher up, and spoke with some vehemence about the dangers of our spending too much time with troublemakers who really didn't represent anybody of significance and could give us wrong views. But I sensed his heart was not entirely in what he was saying. He said he himself knew the people in question quite well and saw them from time to time. He later turned out to be quite close to some of those high in the opposition. I did not commit myself to any change in practice.

Meanwhile the Pentagon official was stirring things up in Washington; there was some publicity, and I was getting queries from home base. I laid out to the State Department the full case for the range of contacts the embassy had and, so far as I was concerned, would continue to have, while I stressed that we would try to achieve a broad balance among government, supporters of the regime, and the democratic opposition. The working level of the department endorsed what we were doing. The official for whom the luncheon had been arranged sent me a rather cool note saying he wished it all hadn't happened. I would guess he was a bit concerned about his bureaucratic flanks, particularly in a situation in which he was not certain what Secretary Kissinger's reaction might be. In Madrid, we continued as we were.

I am a strong believer in the importance of the human factor in diplomacy. Development of personal relationships of confidence is a vital part of the effective conduct of foreign relations. It takes time and effort, and depends to a greater degree on honesty, openness, and a genuine interest in understanding than is generally appreciated. It also requires patience and a clear separation of the important from the picayune. It is no substitute for a basic coincidence of national interests, but it can greatly assist in keeping that coincidence of interests to the forefront and in preventing small problems from ballooning into big ones. The building of such relationships of confidence with knowledgeable and key or potentially key people is one of the principal reasons for having diplomatic representation abroad.

Spain in 1974 and 1975 was on the verge of a sweeping change of guard. New leaders were waiting in the wings to take over. They were accessible and impressionable. The personal relations developed in Spain during this period with young men who were then in the shadows between political illegitimacy and legitimacy, but who were later to become key personages in their country's politics and policies, were therefore of special significance to the longer-term conduct of US-Spanish relations. One of these young Spaniards acknowledged as much when I called on him in his new job as an undersecretary in King Juan Carlos's first government in December 1975. He said: "There is one thing I want you to know. We may not always agree. We may take different positions at times. But I will always remember how you and your government kept in touch with me when I was in opposition, and that will always be a consideration in our dealings."

THE NEW KING 3

The strongest political force in Spain at the moment of Franco's death was the idea of democracy. Even before his death it was arguable, despite the degree of control he still was demonstrating, whether his time had not in fact already passed and the time of political liberalization come. Among the portents of liberalization were the efforts of Manuel Fraga and Pio Cabanillas for greater press freedom when they were in the Ministry of Information together at the beginning of the 1970s. Portentous, too, were the attempts—abortive though they then were—to begin "political associations." The persistence in 1974 and 1975 of Prime Minister Arias, despite his long-proven loyalty to Franco, in his efforts to give life to the Spirit of February 12, and the minor successes he achieved, were new and stronger symptoms of the inexorability of political change in the Spain of that time. The change that was already occurring, although slowly, even with Franco, was bound to occur more decidedly and more rapidly now without him.

This central fact was clear to everyone except the most obdurate or the most poorly informed, in spite of the outpouring of emotion that occurred upon Franco's death and during the funeral and burial proceedings in the days that followed. The old warrior was being honored by some—even many—for the exceptional leader of Spain that he had been—whether you hated him or loved him, liked what he had done or despised it.

DEMOCRATIZATION: HOW FAST, AND HOW FAR?

The differences among Spaniards even in those final days of Franco were not over whether democratization would occur, but rather over how—at what pace and with what consequences. The moderate Francoists, including such men as President of the Cortes Rodríguez de Valcárcel and Prime Minister Arias, accepted the idea that there should be political change. At the same time they were concerned that it not go too far too fast—that it not go against the socially, politically, and economically conservative principles laid down by Franco.

At the other end of the democratic spectrum, the Socialists were concerned that the change might not go far enough—to include them, for instance, among legitimate political groups participating in the process—or fast enough, since there was a danger that their followers might become radicalized through impatience and frustration. Their concern was shared by a number of informed observers, including a leading figure in the Spanish church with whom I spoke during those days. He told me he was afraid the whole process would break down and there would be chaos unless democratization were achieved within six months. Although I well understood the need to move steadily toward the democratic objective, I could not understand, and did not believe in, his six-month deadline. To me it represented a lack of appreciation of the many and complex institutional, juridical, and personnel changes that had to be made in the process. Rather, there was a need to negotiate the changes in a democratic way that would assure broad acceptance; they could not be imposed in one fell swoop. Four years later, with the negotiations still in process but a generally admitted success so far, the six-month limit specified by this churchman had been demonstrated to have been highly unrealistic.

The bulk of the Spanish population was, indeed, ambivalent about political change. On the one hand most of them wanted it, as was to be later demonstrated by their votes in a referendum and in elections. On the other hand, they did not want a degree of change that would place in jeopardy either the quite extraordinary material progress they had achieved over the past fifteen years or the general sense of order and security that most of them, except in the Basque country, felt.

The stereotype of Spain in much of Europe and the United States at the time was of a still poor, backward, agricultural country given to passion and violence—the country of Hemingway. The popular reaction in Europe and the United States upon Franco's death tended to be twofold: relief that the last Western European dictator had gone; and anticipation—given the Spanish history and temperament—that conflict, violence, and political extremes would be the almost inevitable sequel. This bias carried over to the political leaders. When it was coupled with the emphasis, in the minds of the principal leaders of the United States during this time, on maintaining a strong security relationship, the result was predictable. The official position of the United States was to support the process of political liberalization in Spain under the King, but with a more-than-evident note of caution, in some conversations at high levels, regarding the pace of that liberalization. This note of caution was particularly apparent in the early days, immediately after Franco's death. It was less pronounced, however, as time passed and as more experience was gained with modern Spain and its leading personalities. I shall return to this point later.

The King Takes a Hand. In this situation of ambivalence both within Spain and outside regarding the desirable degree and pace of political liberalization, it was the new young King who would be the arbiter. He would be, as Foreign Minister Areilza was soon to say (although perhaps without much conviction at the time), the motor of change. But no one knew this for sure when Franco died and Juan Carlos became chief of state. Until then he had been completely in Franco's shadow.

Juan Carlos was born in Rome and brought to Spain for the first time at ten years of age in 1948, to be educated. He was taught in a series of Spanish military schools, in which he did well. He mastered Portuguese, Italian, and French in addition to Spanish; became an avid sportsman; married a very attractive lady who was exceptionally well prepared for her new position as Princess of Spain; and learned, at Franco's side but two steps to the rear, to be prudent and to participate in ceremonial functions. He did nothing to distinguish himself particularly or to presage how strong he would be or what he would try to achieve once he became King. We knew that he was impatient to take over and that he believed in political liberalization, but we did not know how well developed his thinking was, what specifically he had in mind, or how forcefully and effectively he would lead.

The central political question in Spain at that juncture was, then, not whether there should be political liberalization, but rather how fast and how far it should go and in what manner it should be accomplished. The moderate Francoists said it should be slowly, deliberately, within limits well defined by the conservative principles of the Franco period, and under the continuing control of the proven leaders of the past—the "bunker" as they were graphically dubbed by the political commentators of Spain. The democratic opposition on the left said it should be more rapidly, with a sweeping away of many of the institutions and many of the customs of the past, and with the full participation of all significant political forces, under new, younger, more dynamic leadership. Franco, Juan Carlos's political mentor, would have had the young King follow the first route. He thought he had prepared the way for him to do so, or, anyway, he said he thought so. He said that when he died everything would be "well tied down" (*atado y bién atado*). Don Juan, the young king's father but also still his rival for power, would have had him follow the second route. To the surprise of many, Juan Carlos in the end came closer to his father's route. But he had learned enough from Franco about the virtues of patience and prudence and the art of manipulation, and he understood—or was concerned by—the dynamics of Spain's political situation sufficiently not to hurry the pace too much. Thus the first seven months of his reign were a time of testing the waters and of preliminary positioning for what would be done later.

To manage and administer the change as he wished, the King needed his own men: men in whom he had personal confidence, men whose beliefs corresponded to his, men who would follow his lead, men of his own generation where possible. He would try to surround himself with such men in due course, but initially he would concentrate on a few key positions. He retained as his closest personal aide and chief of his household the Marqués de Mondejar, an elderly retired military man who had been with him, assisted him, and counseled him for years. But Mondejar was not a political figure in a position of political power. The three key political posts were president of the Cortes, prime minister of the government, and deputy prime minister for defense affairs. The King concentrated first on getting his man as president of the Cortes. That man was Torcuato Fernández Miranda, an able, rather dour product of the Franco regime who had risen to be acting prime minister briefly in the period between the death of Carrero Blanco and the assumption of the prime ministership by Arias. The King was attracted especially to him because he knew him well (he had been the King's tutor at one point), had absolute confidence in his loyalty and his ability, and knew he favored political liberalization (although probably not of the type and degree the King had ultimately in mind) and could devise ways of maneuvering liberalization past the Francoist institutions and personalities that still abounded. By fortunate coincidence the position of president of the Cortes was just coming open. The term of the incumbent, conservative Francoist Alejandro Rodríguez de Valcárcel, was about to end. But getting agreement to Fernández Miranda for the job did not turn out to be easy. He was not well liked as a personality. Considerable resistance developed. It is reported that the King achieved his objective only through the help of Prime Minister Arias, a man he was thinking of firing. This says something about the degree to which the King had to depend on others to achieve his purposes in those early days of his reign.

The King's second priority among the key political positions was the prime ministership. It is clear he would have preferred an immediate change from Arias to someone closer and more responsive to him. He seems to have favored a former Franco minister of industry, José María López de Letona. But the difficulty he had in achieving his objective in the appointment of Fernández Miranda to the presidency of the Cortes led him to decide on the continuance of Arias for the time being.

The position of deputy prime minister for defense affairs was a newly created one, reflecting the King's understanding of the critical importance to his success of the support, or at least the acquiescence, of the military. For this position, the King probably would have liked to turn immediately to another former tutor in whom he had great confidence, General Manuel Gutiérrez Mellado. But Gutiérrez Mellado had not yet been promoted to the rank of lieutenant general and would not have had broad acceptance among the top military officers. Therefore the King opted for a more senior officer who was a logical choice from the military hierarchy's point of view, the very conservative Lieutenant General Fernando de Santiago y Díaz de Mendivil.

Thus for the top three political positions the King had to content himself in the first round with only one appointee who was his personal preference. However, this was the key spot from his point of view. Fernández Miranda would help him inestimably in bureaucratic maneuver as president of the Cortes and subsequently, from his other position as president of the Council of the Realm, in the naming of Juan Carlos's personal choice as prime minister. Meanwhile, the King would receive further support from other cabinet members for what he wanted to achieve and would have an opportunity to observe their performance as he prepared for the next phase.

The other outstanding members of the cabinet were three. Manuel Fraga, named minister of government, was a dynamic, overwhelming personality in his early fifties who as a Franco minister of information had shown liberalizing tendencies. José María Areilza, an articulate, urbane, cultured, ambitious man in his mid-sixties, had been ambassador to the United States, France, and Argentina under Franco, then had broken with him and become a confidant of Don Juan and a member of the opposition who had contacts with the Left. Areilza was named foreign minister. Antonio Garrigues, a distinguished elder lawyer, Catholic layman, and former ambassador to the United States who favored political liberalization, became minister of justice.

Two young men with potential for the future were Minister of the Presidency Alfonso Osorio and Minister of the Movement Adolfo Suárez, the latter said to have been suggested for the job by Torcuato Fernández Miranda. The National Movement had been Franco's vehicle for articulation of his regime's political views, for mobilizing support, and for dispensation of patronage. It was formed in the 1950s to replace the Falange and other groups supporting Franco after the name Falange, with the victory of the Allies over the Axis, had become an embarrassment. Over time it had developed a large, nationwide bureaucracy charged with proselytizing, fund raising, keeping tabs on local events, and providing certain social benefits. Besides much property, it had extensive radio and press operations. It was not a bad place from which to establish political lines and gain political experience.

The King had now made his first principal personnel choices. He also made it clear in his first speeches that he expected to be King of all Spaniards and to preside over a Spain in which all Spaniards had a say in their government. He then concentrated over the next few months on building his own image during trips throughout Spain and also on two urgent foreign policy matters, Spanish Sahara and the treaty with the United States.

The trips around the country were very successful. He and his personable and charming queen, Sofía, were a handsome, attractive couple whose graciousness and interest in their people were there for all to see. The experience of the Spanish people with Alfonso XIII had not predisposed them to favor a return to monarchy, but the conduct and appearance of the King and the Queen as they traveled around the country, and as they went about their official obligations and daily routine in Madrid, added to their personal popularity and gave the monarchy a more solid base. It became better known that Juan Carlos was not one to stand on ceremony and wanted concrete things done in response to his people's needs. It became better known that Sofía, as well as being a lovely person with a winning smile, was a devoted mother who also had a continuing intellectual curiosity. She personally occupied herself with the care of their children and continued to attend a class on comparative religion at the University of Madrid. The three children, two girls and eight-year-old Prince Felipe, completed an ideal family picture.

Stories began to go the rounds about the King and the Queen, stories that were appreciated by Spaniards, who were looking for greater youth, warmth, compassion, and informality and found them in their new sovereigns. Two of these stories were as follows.

The King liked to sail a good sailboat, drive a good car, fly his own helicopter, and sometimes—it was said—ride his own motorcycle. On one such occasion, he was buzzing along incognito on a highway near Madrid in the evening when he noticed another young man at the side of the road beside a motorcycle stalled for lack of gas. The King stopped and offered help. The young man did not recognize him with his helmet on and in the darkness. He got on the back of the King's motorcycle, and the King took him to the nearest gas station. There the King took off his helmet for a moment and the young man suddenly recognized him. He was profuse in his apologies, thanked the King for what he had done, and assumed the King would then go on his way. The King would have nothing of that. He insisted on taking the young man back to his motorcycle with his can of gasoline, and on making sure he was well on his way again. The King then resumed his nocturnal outing.

The Queen wanted her children to live as normal a life as possible and to have contact with other children of their age. She took much personal interest in their day-to-day activities. One Saturday, the story goes, eight-year-old Felipe was very down in the mouth. She asked him what the trouble was. He explained that his friend, Jaime, was having a birthday party to which all his other classmates had been invited but he had not. He could not understand why and he was upset. His mother promptly called Jaime's mother, said it was Sofía and told her the problem. When Jaime's mother realized it was the Queen calling, she quickly explained she had simply assumed it would not be appropriate to invite the young Prince. Sofía said it would and asked her the favor of inviting Felipe so that his day would not be spoiled. Jaime's mother readily agreed, and Queen Sofía personally drove young Felipe to the party.

A favorable image was emerging; the monarchy was thus being strengthened.

Foreign Policy: Spanish Sahara and the Green March. In foreign affairs, both the negotiations with the United States and the signing of the treaty could be completed expeditiously. A framework agreement had already been signed by Foreign Minister Cortina and Secretary Kissinger before Franco's death, and it was the first major public document the King had signed while he was acting chief of state during Franco's last illness. Now the King wanted to have the agreement with the United States completed quickly, provided it could be upgraded in form and in content. This was done and a treaty, not an executive agreement, was signed in January 1976.

The Sahara, Spain's other most urgent foreign policy issue at this time, was more complicated and controversial. Spain had long ago made the basic policy decision to get out of Spanish Sahara, which was its last colonial territory. The attempt to stay was not worth the financial and political drain, despite the wealth of the recently developed phosphate deposits in that large but sparsely populated area. The problem was not whether to get out but how to do so with honor. Spain wanted to be sure the largely nomadic population of Spanish Sahara, which probably numbered only about seventy-five thousand at the time, was properly consulted. This and Spain's orderly exit might not have been difficult, with the help of the United Nations, which had been involved in the issue for some years, except that Morocco was making insistent claims to the territory—claims actively disputed by Algeria and also by an Algerian-supported group in the Sahara called the POLISARIO (Front for the Liberation of Al-Saguia, Al-Hamura, and Rio de Oro).

During Franco's last illness, King Hassan of Morocco forced the issue by organizing the so-called Green March of civilians on Morocco. The Green March was an innovative device for achieving occupation of Spanish Sahara under circumstances that made resistance by a foe that valued its relations with the invading country especially difficult. After all, firing on invading soldiers to turn them back would be one thing, but firing on the civilians of the Green March would be quite another. It could not help but fuel the emotions of Morocco and affect its political stance for decades. What Spain wanted above all else was to avoid a debilitating fight at that time. The experience of Portugal, trying to defend its last colonial holdings too long, was close at hand and fresh in mind to reinforce this determination. Thus Spain bowed to the pressure applied by Morocco and negotiated the Madrid Accords. Under these accords, by Spain's interpretation, its administrative control of Spanish Sahara, but not its sovereignty over that area (which was not its to give anyway), passed to Morocco. The Green March was terminated, and Spain was permitted an orderly departure of its military and other personnel from Spanish Sahara without bloodshed. The process of negotiating these accords was begun while Franco was still alive but was completed under the King. It was not completed, however, without a dramatic gesture on the King's part. As one of his first acts after becoming King, and over the opposition of Prime Minister Arias and other members of the cabinet, he flew to Spanish Sahara and appeared before the Spanish troops there to show that he supported them and to say that it was his intent to be "the first soldier of Spain." This action did not change the end result of Spanish withdrawal without a fight; in fact, it seemed contradictory to Spain's firm resolve to withdraw. Nevertheless, it symbolized the King's sensitivity to matters affecting the spirit and morale of the Spanish military—a sensitivity born of long experience with the military through his attendance at the military schools of the three services and frequent continuing contacts with the military thereafter. It also reflected his full understanding of how important it would be for the military to accept his leadership as chief of state.

Problems with Arias. The King's activities during this first phase of his reign—image building through travel and his modest role in foreign affairs— did not center on matters of his choice. He doubtless would have liked to be more continuously and deeply involved in internal matters, and to have pushed the process of political liberalization forward more rapidly and more decisively. However, Prime Minister Arias considered the modalities of this process to be very much *his* responsibility. Arias consequently went his own deliberate and cautious way with relatively little reference to the King. In response to popular pressure, an amnesty for certain political prisoners was granted in December, but reliable reports were that the amnesty was much more limited than the King would have wished. After what seemed an unduly long delay, Arias delivered a speech in February outlining his new plans for political liberalization now that Franco had died. They were disappointingly imprecise, and cloaked in Franco-period rhetoric. They included modification of the penal code, liberalization of the law of assembly and of the law of politial association, and elaboration of a new electoral law; there would in due course be a referendum to determine the people's will with regard to democratization, but the specific nature and timing of this referendum were not stated. All these measures were necessary. They might also have been sufficient had it been clear they would be unrestrictive in their nature and, moreover, vigorously promoted by Arias. Neither was clear. He seemed overly committed to doing things through traditional institutions and leaders who could not be counted on to favor the degree and pace of progress required. For instance, he still could not even bring himself to use the phrase "political parties" instead of that euphemism for Francoist ears, "political associations." He continually invoked the past and the image of Franco. His attitude gave support to those who advocated rupture (*ruptura*) with the past since reform (*reforma*) through existing institutions seemed too slow and uncertain so long as he was there. He was thus a polarizing influence so far as the Center Left and Left were concerned, while he tried to placate the Right. Moreover, he would not go to the King for guidance and support. In fact, he sent his basic February policy speech to the King in the most pro forma of ways, only at the last minute before it was to be delivered. The King certainly could not be very happy with this mode of operation.

Meanwhile, the two strongest men in the King's first government, Minister of Government Fraga and Foreign Minister Areilza, were projecting images of dynamism and activity that went beyond the normal confines of their functions. Both made frequent public statements on the desirable nature of political reform and on the calendar that should be followed. Fraga alternately made such liberal moves as permitting the socialist-allied trade union, the General Union of Workers (UGT), to hold its first public meeting in Spain since the 1930s, and such restrictive ones as having some moderate Christian Democrats arrested while consorting with others farther to the left in an unauthorized political meeting. He thus seemed to be playing to both the Left and the Right. Areilza traveled throughout Europe advertising the new Spanish vocation for democracy and making statements about what should be done that went beyond what Arias had in mind. Arias soon became quite disenchanted with Areilza's freewheeling and took steps to limit his rhetoric. To say that the two men were basically incompatible politically and temperamentally would be the neatest of understatements. This was well publicized and hurt Areilza not at all in the eyes of those impatient for more rapid and decisive action, while further damaging Arias' deteriorating image.

What a difference a year could make! A year previously, in another context, Arias had seemed a persistent advocate of political liberalization determinedly pressing a reluctant Franco for the freedom to carry out a meaningful though modest program of political reform. Now he seemed an uncertain, indecisive figure with little taste for the game, and suspicious and distrustful of his cabinet colleagues. What had happened? In part, the explanation doubtless was that during Franco's lifetime Arias was prepared to fight the good fight for modest reform because he knew it must come and because he also knew Franco was still there to prevent it from going what he and other Francoists considered too far too fast. Now his situation was entirely different. He was being pressed to go faster and farther than he had planned, and he had no blueprint for that. He had not thought his plan of action through, and the threat to his position was now not restraint from the Right but rather the push from the Left to overstep the bounds that would have been imposed in the past. Moreover, in spite of the fact that Arias had pressed Franco to move faster and farther than Franco had wished, he was immensely loyal to Franco's memory. Finally, his impressions of the young King were from the past, when Juan Carlos had been a junior ceremonial figure in the background; indeed, there was over twenty years' difference in their ages. Arias could not help but think of Juan Carlos even now as an inexperienced young man who should be kept safely away from the serious day-to-day business of government. He was more comfortable working with the leaders of the Right, who were of his generation, who had inherited Franco's ideas, and who still held many of the reins of power. He was working with them in his own way—to some extent effectively so—to move the political reform process along, but slowly, indecisively, unconvincingly, and without contact with the Left. He was, in fact, thinking himself of forming a political party of what he called the Center. But the times, the real political map of Spain that he did not divine, and the King would not permit prolonged continuance of his hesitant tack, governed as it was by a course set in obeisance to the nostalgic Right.*

Arias's lack of decisiveness and forcefulness in the new situation, his inability to talk with the Left, and his unwillingness to look to the throne for leadership were not lost on the King. Juan Carlos had not wanted him to continue as prime minister in the first place, but had been forced to temporize because the opposition to his first priority appointment, that of Torcuato Fernández Miranda as president of the Cortes, had been so great. He now felt he must have a new prime minister. Private and to some degree public speculation about an imminent change grew. In April 1976 the King's dissatisfaction with Arias spilled over into public print in an interview with Arnaud de Borchgrave published in *Newsweek*. In May a leading politician lunching with me and the embassy's political counselor told us, presumably

---

*What the real political map turns out to be is described at the end of chapter 4.

on his own initiative, that the King had to make a change of prime minister to get the political reform effort moving, and that he should be given support to this end during his forthcoming visit to the United States. Our response was that such matters were entirely up to the King and Spain to decide. Clearly the United States supported the King and political liberalization in Spain, but it could not, should not, and would not involve itself in the specifics of what was to be done with regard to either policies or personalities. Moreover, it would not be good for Spain for a change of prime minister, if that were to occur, to appear to be made in the United States.

The New Prime Minister. There was a growing feeling in Madrid that Arias should leave office and would soon do so. But if he went who would replace him? The two most obvious candidates were Fraga and Areilza. Fraga was more attractive to the Right because of his forceful personality and tough stand on public order. He had kept the streets well under control when the effervescence of the first post-Franco days might have boiled over into them. He had been burned somewhat by a violent encounter among Carlists in Vitoria that he had not seemed to anticipate and plan for well enough. He had seemed to go too far in some political arrests. Nevertheless, he certainly was more of a liberalizer as well as a stronger, more decisive personality than Arias. Areilza was an energetic man of impressive presence and silver tongue in several languages; his break with Franco in the latter's final years, as well as his contacts with the Left, gave him stronger credentials with Leftists than Fraga but made him anathema to the Right, including the military. In the end there was another factor that worked decisively against either of these obvious candidates: they were both of an older generation than the King's, and each was of such strong personality that the King could not have counted upon either to have been as responsive to his will as he desired at this critical juncture in Spanish history.

So he looked for a younger man of or near to his own generation who would be more responsive to him. Previously he had thought of López de Letona; but López de Letona had since slipped into the background. Now two young politicians had come to the fore: Alfonso Osorio, as minister of the prime ministership; and Adolfo Suárez, as minister of the movement. Osorio was a Christian Democrat who had held responsible government and private business jobs. Suárez had made no mistakes in the seven months since Franco's death. He had filled in capably for Fraga during the latter's absence from the country. He had used his position as minister-secretary general of the movement to plant some of his own men in key political spots, competing with Fraga in this regard. And he had given a widely applauded speech before the Cortes in defense of the bill liberalizing the provisions of the political associations law (he said that the government had the responsibility for consolidating democracy, and that it must start with the recognition of a pluralistic society). He had come up through the ranks of the Franco political system, but he now spoke like a liberalizer. He was relatively unknown publicly, but he was well known to the King, with whom he had managed to have frequent contact for a number of years. Moreover, Torcuato Fernández Miranda, the King's closest official advisor, favored him.

In June 1976 the King went on his visit to the United States, where he made a convincing impression in his speech before a joint session of Congress and otherwise as a personable young leader committed to the democratization of his country. Whether he talked with anyone in the United States during this time about his plan to change his prime minister, I do not know. If he did, I doubt that much more was said to him other than that it was his decision to make. What he did receive was a psychological lift from the warm reception he found wherever he went in the United States. He was to refer to this in a most positive way some two years later when I took a visiting congressional group to see him. The King said then that few people knew or could understand how much the fine reception he had in the United States had meant to him. He came back to Spain feeling more confident and more resolved than ever to continue on the course he had set for himself.

Three weeks later—long enough to avoid any connection between his action and his trip to the United States—the King called in Prime Minister Arias and asked for and received his resignation. He then asked the president of the Council of the Realm, Fernández Miranda, to obtain from the council a panel of three names for him (as the process of naming a new Prime Minister required) that would include Adolfo Suárez. While most of Spain and most Spain-watchers elsewhere speculated over the names of Areilza, Fraga, and some others, the Council of the Realm took its time in deliberation. Finally, Fernández Miranda emerged from a council meeting with the enigmatic remark, "I am prepared to give the King what he has asked for." The next day, July 3, 1976, the King named Suárez to form a new government.

THE **KING GAMBLES** 4

King Juan Carlos took a historic gamble in removing Arias from the prime ministership and appointing Adolfo Suárez. He gambled not only in changing from an experienced politician—one who combined protective links to the Right with a certain record of commitment to political change—to a relative political unknown who had not demonstrated his ability to lead at this level. He also gambled (more fundamentally, although this was not immediately apparent to outside observers) in switching from a political strategy based primarily on gradual persuasion of the Right to one based primarily on dialogue and compromise with the Center Left and Left.

In so gambling, he placed himself and the monarchy far out on a limb. He well recognized this, and was prepared to take the risk. The editor of a leading Spanish magazine with whom I had lunch a week after the change, quoted him to me as saying he realized that his standing in the public eye, which was at its highest after his successful visit to the United States, would decline, but he would work hard to rebuild it. His success in this regard would depend very much on how well Suárez did. He was also quoted to the effect that he was not "married to Suárez"—implicit recognition of the inevitable day when, in a parliamentary democracy, he would have and work with a different prime minister. Nevertheless, the fact was that in July 1976 the King laid a great part of his future fortunes on the line with Suárez and with the new political approach, stressing an opening to the left, that he and Suárez together would work out over the coming months.

THE SUÁREZ GOVERNMENT

At first the appointment of Suárez was most disconcerting to political observers and to participants in the political process in Spain. A leading

Spanish reformist and political commentator speculated in his first column after the change that this might mean a step backward in the democratization process. He doubtless was influenced by Suárez's youth and lack of stature and by the fact that he had come up through the ranks of Franco's political bureaucracy and, in fact, most recently had been minister of the movement. He was soon to be proven wrong in his speculation, but his first reaction testified to the general uncertainty over Suárez's credentials at the outset. It also testified to a feeling that Arias's performance and prospects were not as hopeless as they were later described as having been.

The uncertainty over Suárez's credentials, as well as the unwillingness of some other putative candidates for the prime ministership to accept him as their leader, is also demonstrated by the difficulty the King and Suárez encountered in making up a new government. Fraga and Areilza quickly decided they did not want to continue. Neither did Antonio Garrigues. Two Fraga men, Minister of Education Robles Piquer and Minister of Information Adolfo Martín Gamero, went with Fraga, and a leading Christian Democrat, Fernando Alvarez de Miranda, declined a ministry, as did Spain's leading economist, Enrique Fuentes Quintana. Fuentes later told me he declined because he did not think Suárez would have the strength and will to take the economic actions that were necessary. His choice at that time would have been Fraga. A year later, by which time he was playing a very constructive role in economic policy, he had a different view.

The cabinet that was formed comprised a mixture of a few holdovers, mainly in the military ministries, and a large number of relative unknowns, many of them quite young. The King had now achieved the second of his personnel priorities—the first, it will be remembered, was the naming of Torcuato Fernández Miranda as president of the Cortes—by getting his own man as prime minister. But he had considerably shaken the political structure and confidence of the country in the process. Therefore, he was not prepared further to roil the waters at that moment by taking the next step: changes in the military command. Thus Lieutenant General Fernando de Santiago y Díaz de Mendivil continued for the time being as first vice-president for defense affairs, and the ministers of army, navy, and air continued without change. Alfonso Osorio remained in the cabinet and was elevated to vice-president for political affairs. Five other members of the cabinet who were to stand out in the future but who were not so well known then were Rodolfo Martín Villa as minister of interior, Landelino Lavilla as minister of justice, Marcelino Oreja as minister of foreign affairs, Leopoldo Calvo Sotelo as minister of public works, and Fernando Abril Martorell as minister of agriculture. All these five men were in their thirties or early forties. Martín Villa had held the most responsible public position previously, having been a successful civil governor of Barcelona. Lavilla's highest public position had been undersecretary of industry. Oreja was Areilza's undersecretary of foreign affairs. Abril Martorell had worked closely with Suárez when the latter was civil governor of Segovia, but had had no previous position of importance in the central government.

The principal tasks facing Suárez and his government were to establish new momentum in the democratization process and to demonstrate that, despite the government's overall youth and inexperience, it could in fact govern effectively. New momentum toward democracy was accomplished through a strong statement of democratic intent at the outset; through the adoption of a liberal, politically pragmatic approach to the controversial and thorny amnesty issue; through the initiation of a quite remarkable dialogue with the Left, a dialogue that led ultimately to fuller participation by the Left in the political process than anyone would have anticipated; and, over the course of a year, through the holding of, first, a successful national referendum on democratization and, second, Spain's first free national legislative elections in forty years. The new government established a credible image of effectiveness by its extraordinarily hard work in the dogged elaboration of practical solutions to the multitude of problems and issues that arose daily along an uncharted route. A major factor in its success was the strong personal leadership of Suárez, who insisted on knowing every issue thoroughly and making all important decisions himself, after due consultation with the King.

The government's introductory statement of democratic intent was characterized in these words by a leading political commentator:

> If a year ago anyone had drafted a political manifesto which assured that sovereignty resides in the people; that there would be respect for political groups; that the government would come from a majority, democratically determined in free election; and that there would be freedom of expression, he would at this moment have been on trial and in need of the amnesty that the government is about to grant.*

Amnesty and Terrorism. It will be remembered that the Arias government had granted a limited amnesty in December 1975, immediately after Juan Carlos became King, but that it had been generally considered inadequate. The Suárez government set about devising and putting into effect a sweeping further amnesty immediately after it took office in July 1976. As described to me by the undersecretary of justice, this new amnesty was to achieve, through judicial action in each individual case, the early release of 370 of the some 500 political prisoners then in jail. In time, most of the political prisoners who remained in jail might have their sentences further reduced if terrorist actions died down. In addition, some 500 prisoners in

---

*Luis Apostúa, *YA,* July 18, 1976.

jail for contravention of military regulations would be released, including about 200 conscientious objectors and 200 deserters. He explained that the military had decided that any action taken with regard to conscientious objectors should logically extend to deserters.

This broad amnesty was well received and defused the pressures in this regard for a time. But before elections were held in June 1977 the political pressures for release of all so-called political prisoners again became so strong that the government felt obliged to take two further steps and in the end to release virtually all such prisoners, including some of those convicted of assassination or complicity in assassination. In March 1977 the government broadened the July 1976 amnesty. When even that did not calm the protests from the Basque country, the government released in early June 1977 most remaining Basque prisoners accused of committing crimes having political ends, with the most controversial prisoners being sent into exile. The government took these further steps despite the fact that terrorist acts had continued in the meantime. Prime examples were the assassination of the president of the Guipuzcoa Municipal Assembly, Juan María de Araluce, on October 4, 1976; the kidnappings of the president of the Council of State, Antonio Oriol, on December 10, 1976, and the president of the Supreme Military Justice Council, General Emilio Villaescusa, on January 24, 1977 (both were eventually released through police action); and the assassination of two armed policemen and one civil guard on January 28. The government acted as it did so that the elections would be completely unmarred by any accusations of continuing vestiges of past political repression, and to assure as full and favorable Basque electoral participation as possible.

Dialogue with the Left. Generous amnesties were, of course, only a small part of the process of achieving full participation in the political process. A much greater part was the opening of a dialogue between the government and the Left, something that would have been unthinkable for Arias to have undertaken. In a few months this dialogue led to accepting the Socialists as legitimate participants in the political game and persuading them to play that game in a moderate, cooperative fashion (actions that would also have been anathema to Arias); reaching a decision on legalization of the Communist Party, a potential move so radical it had scarcely been discussed in the Madrid of summer 1976; and persuading the Right to accept all these extraordinary departures from past practice.

Suárez began by holding lengthy and well-publicized private sessions with the young Socialist leader Felipe González Márquez (he was thirty-seven), during which they both learned that they could at least talk with each other and that there might be a basis for working out compromises on specific issues as they arose. His government proceeded from there to looking the other way while the still technically illegal Socialist Workers Party (PSOE) held an open congress in Madrid from December 5 to 8, 1976; it was attended by such Western European social democratic luminaries as Willy Brandt, François Mitterrand, Olaf Palme, and Pietro Nenni. Then, in early February 1977, the government issued a decree-law that abolished the existing machinery for registering political parties—machinery that had involved too much government discretion to be acceptable to the Socialists—in favor of an administrative procedure. This opened the way for the prompt legalization of all major political parties except the Communist Party, and even it immediately presented its application for registration as a legal party. All this was accomplished not simply as if by preconceived detailed plan, but rather through slow, tortuous dialogue and compromise as each complex issue was faced, worried over, and then finally resolved. The resulting full participation of the PSOE in the political process was in dramatic contrast to the recent past when its leaders had been in jail, in exile, or underground, and when no public reference to any political party—much less the PSOE—was permissible.

LEGALIZING THE COMMUNISTS

The legalization of the Spanish Communist Party (PCE) was not really a larger issue than that of bringing the Socialists into the political process, considering the relative vote-drawing power of the two parties and the still radical rhetoric of some of the PSOE leadership. But it was more controversial, and it was filled with drama that could scarcely have been exceeded in fiction.

Santiago Carrillo, secretary general of the PCE since 1960, had been in exile for years in Paris. Over the years, he had begun to take a more independent line with regard to the Soviet Union, and he had sharply criticized its 1968 intervention in Czechoslovakia. He was reported to have returned to Spain from time to time clandestinely. In the latter part of 1976 the possibility of permitting him to return openly was being discussed; the most common position was that this would not, and should not, happen, if only because the government could not guarantee his safety from assassination by the Right and the consequent creation of a martyr for the extreme Left. Moreover, the military certainly would not stand for his roaming around Spain freely and participating in politics. The principal arguments then used for his return and open participation in the political process were that the myth of communist strength would be thus deflated, that there could be no deprecation of the eventual elections on the grounds that a significant political group had been excluded, and that the Communists would be weaker out in the open than underground. In addition, the Socialists were pressing for legalization of the Communist Party, and if they were to carry out their threat not to participate in the political process because the Communists were excluded the legitimacy of any elections held would be called into question and the European democracies would continue their reluctance to accept Spain.*

On July 28, 1976, the PCE Central Committee met openly in Rome, and Spain's leading labor leader of the Left, Marcelino Camacho, was publicly revealed to be a member of it, as was a well-known left-leaning economist, Ramón Tamames. Then suddenly, on December 10, Carrillo dramatically confirmed his ability to travel into and out of Spain in disguise by holding a clandestine press conference in Madrid; and on December 22 he was arrested in Madrid, wearing a wig as a thin disguise. It was not entirely clear at that point who was more interested in Carrillo's being arrested: the police or Carrillo himself. He was a hot potato for the police, and his arrest brought the question of his being in Spain to a head at a convenient time for him.

On December 30 Carrillo was released from jail, on bail, and the question of whether he should be permitted to return to Spain had been effectively answered. Later, Dolores Ibarruri, the famous La Pasionaria of Civil War days and a long-time PCE leader, was also able to return from Russia where she had lived for years.

Now, in February 1977, came the follow-on question of whether the PCE should be legalized. There were a variety of legal arguments, but the practical political arguments were the same as before. On the one hand, legalization might polarize the Right, be intolerable to the military, and give the Communists freedom they could effectively use over time to destabilize democracy and eventually take over themselves. On the other hand, legalization would bring them out in the open, reveal dramatically their electoral weakness (as it had for the Communists in Portugal), diminish their real ability to do mischief, and remove a pretext for claiming the elections were not fully representative. To complicate matters, a Eurocommunist summit was held in Madrid on March 2 and 3; it was attended by Enrico Berlinguer from Italy and Georges Marchais from France and

---

*As it later turned out, there were two other arguments. First, after the PCE's legalization the PSOE, which had at one time joined the PCE in an uncomfortable tactical alliance of the Left called the Platajunta, no longer felt obliged to support the cause of the PCE in any way. In fact, the PSOE and the PCE began bitter competition when both were allowed full political participation. Second, Carrillo and the PCE, permitted to participate openly and fully in the political process, provided the government with valuable support on issues of public order and economic stabilization.

seemed to show Carrillo as the most advanced of these three Eurocommunists in terms of willingness to criticize the Soviet Union and its system.

The government responded to the challenge of the PCE's February application for legalization by turning the issue over to the courts for decision, but this ploy did not work. On March 31 the Supreme Court returned the issue to the government, saying it was not within its jurisdiction. On April 9, Easter Saturday night, with the King out of the country on a trip to Germany, Suárez grasped the nettle firmly, and the government legalized the Spanish Communist Party.*

Military Reactions. A number of top military leaders had not been comfortable from the beginning with the government's opening to the left. In September 1976 General de Santiago, the first vice-president for defense affairs, had resigned because of his opposition to the way things were going. His resignation was accompanied by a letter from him to his military colleagues explaining his position and a supporting open letter by another right-wing general, Carlos Iniesta Cano. The King then appointed in General de Santiago's place the man he had wanted from the beginning, Lieutenant General Manuel Gutiérrez Mellado, and the government responded to what it considered to be the indiscipline of the two generals by attempting to sanction them through early retirement. The latter move ran into resistance and technical snags from within the military, and the government had to draw back. But the critical point for the King, and for Suárez, was that although military opposition had surfaced, the King had been able to make the change at the top of the military that he desired.

The new vice-president for defense affairs was a small, thin, ascetic, disciplined, dedicated Army officer with a reputation for integrity, for liberal political views, and for commitment to military modernization and organizational reform. The former chief of the High General Staff, Lieutenant General Manuel Díez Alegría, who was fired by Franco because he became too prominent, advocated the creation of a Ministry of Defense, and made a well-publicized call on Romanian Prime Minister Ceauşescu, was a close friend and mentor of Gutiérrez Mellado. The latter had worked for Díez Alegría on the High General Staff, and Diéz Alegría once told me that he and Gutiérrez thought exactly alike. Gutiérrez Mellado had also been the principal military member of the Spanish team that negotiated

---

*A colleague told me that the King, upon being advised in Germany of Suárez's action, raised his eyebrows and wondered aloud whether Suárez had done the right thing. I find it difficult to believe, however, that the King and Suárez had not been in close contact in the handling of this important issue, as was their custom, or that they had not reached full agreement on it.

the Treaty of Friendship and Cooperation with the United States. In this position, he was a vehement and tenacious defender of Spanish interests. The King had entertained a special liking and respect for him from the time, in earlier years, when he had been one of his military tutors. The following story is told that illustrates one source of the King's respect. On one occasion, when Gutiérrez Mellado was the young Prince's tutor and was planning a trip to Germany, the Prince asked him to bring back a stereo set for him. This Gutiérrez Mellado did. But when the Prince accepted it and said he would pay him later, Gutiérrez Mellado took it back, saying, "I will give it to you only when you pay for it. A Prince should never owe anyone anything."

The military leadership below the level of Gutiérrez Mellado did not delay in showing its concern over the abrupt legalization of the PCE. On April 12 the High Army Council drafted a statement expressing its displeasure over the legalization, and on April 13 Minister of the Navy Pita da Veiga resigned in protest. The military leaders were not only protesting the action taken. They were also expressing their displeasure with Prime Minister Suárez, who they thought had assured them in a meeting the previous autumn that he would not go this far, and with Gutiérrez Mellado, whom some now began to call "señor" rather than "general" to express their feeling that he had become more of a soft, vacillating, civilian politician than a principled military officer. Feeling among the naval top brass went so deep that the government had trouble finding an admiral who would replace Pita da Veiga as minister of the navy. However, the military went no farther than such verbal and symbolic expressions of their feelings. The top military leaders were disturbed, but they were not prepared to go as far as, for instance, demanding that the King oust Suárez and Gutiérrez Mellado.

The three central principles of the Spanish military had long been national unity, order, and anticommunism. How could they accept without a stronger reaction the clear violation of one of these principles? The explanation doubtless lies partly in the advanced age of most of the military leaders and the fact that their one true leader, Franco, was now gone. But another important part of the explanation is that the Spanish people had so clearly expressed themselves, by general attitude no less than by overwhelming vote in referendum, as giving top priority at this juncture to the democratization process. In fact, this was the essential purpose of the referendum held on the Political Reform Act on December 15, 1976, namely, to demonstrate without doubt to any who would question it that the Spanish people wanted to move ahead with democracy and that other issues meanwhile should be treated as secondary.

A DEMOCRACY IS BORN

The Arias government had been wrestling with the referendum issue—what kind to hold and how—before Arias was replaced. After he had been, the debate continued on whether the proposition presented to the people should be detailed or schematic, on just what it should include, and on whether it should simply be decreed or sent to the Cortes for discussion and approval.

Political and Electoral Reform. The Suárez government and the King eventually decided on a relatively simple Political Reform Act that, upon approval by the Cortes and then the people in referendum, would provide for convocation of elections for a new bicameral Cortes with the authority to write a constitution. The new Cortes would have a Congress of Deputies of 350 members elected by proportional representation, with the number of deputies assigned to provinces according to population (except that each province, no matter how small in population, would have a minimum of three); and a Senate of 207 members elected by plurality, with all but three smaller provinces having four senators. The Congress of Deputies would be the more important and powerful body, but the Senate would have delaying and, in some circumstances, blocking power. The decision to have the act approved by the existing Cortes, which was a holdover from Franco times, was a risky one, opposed by the Left out of fear that this conservative body would effectively emasculate it. But the King and Suárez tested the wind and took the risk, knowing that, if they were successful, their position would be the stronger against eventual rightist opposition for having done so. They were successful. On November 18, 1976, the old Cortes signed its own obituary by approving the political reform bill, and on December 15 the Spanish people in referendum overwhelmingly approved the Political Reform Act.

The King and Suárez had, through their contacts, consultations, and compromises, involved the Left in the ongoing political process to the point that leftist politicians no longer talked about a potentially violent "rupture" with the past but of a nonviolent "rupture by agreement." At the same time, the King and Suárez had now neutralized the Right through the demonstrated will of the people, and even of the politicians of the past, as shown by their favorable votes for the Political Reform Act. These were extraordinary achievements, indeed, and ones that boded well for the future; they provided a solid base and set a framework for democratization. But there was much more to be done. The mechanics and modus operandi for future progress had to be established. An agreed electoral law had to be elaborated and a few coherent political groups capable of participating effectively in elections had to be organized from the hundreds that had formed around coffee tables or over brandy after dinner.

The debate over the electoral law came down to one primarily between the Popular Alliance (AP) on the right, headed by Manuel Fraga, and the parties on the left—the PSOE headed by Felipe González and the PCE headed by Santiago Carrillo—with the government and the several parties of the Center as moderators. The AP wanted a plurality approach, or perhaps even a majority approach accomplished through runoffs, since it was thought this would eliminate splinter groups, favor the AP's prospects and assure more decisive government. The parties of the Left favored pure proportional representation. The compromise adopted in the end was the d'Hondt proportional representation system, which gave opportunities for some minority groups but advantages to the larger parties such that, in the final accounting, splintering would not be a great problem. A further compromise was the provision for a minimum representation of three from each province in the lower house of the legislature. This minimum, adopted at the insistence of the AP, gave conservative agricultural provinces considerably greater representation than would have apportionment purely by population. In the end, the main beneficiary of this provision was not its principal sponsor, the AP, but the coalition of center parties that emerged under Suárez's eventual coalescing leadership.

Party Preparations. Organizing for the elections was a problem for all political parties. After all, none of them had had any experience in this practical side of politics for forty years, and few of them had existing party structures that could produce logical candidates in all provinces by election day. The PSOE and the PCE probably were better off in these regards than the nascent parties of the Center and Right, even though they had operated clandestinely and even though the old National Movement organization could be of help, particularly to whatever party the government backed. But, in truth, even the Left was ill prepared.

In addition to organizational problems, the parties had to make decisions on leadership and identity. On the right, Manuel Fraga characteristically did something early on to resolve the leadership problem. He gathered together six other former Franco ministers whose names and abilities were well known. Together they set out to organize to win the elections for their party, the AP, confident they could do so with the loyal help of former Francoists throughout the country. But the "seven magnificents," as they were dubbed, made a fundamental political error with regard to the AP's identity: they boldly invoked the Franco image and thereby doomed themselves to lose this election before they started. Of course, they also revealed the extent of the electorate's desire for political change.

Many politicians of the Center had hoped that Fraga would be their leader and were greatly disappointed (as, in retrospect he himself may well be) when he turned right. It is interesting to speculate what might have happened had this strong, colorful, and immensely talented if too overwhelming personality had disavowed his Franco heritage and opted for the Center in this period.

The stories about Fraga's ability, and also his intensity and impatience, are legion. Fraga had a history of winning every academic contest he was involved in; of rising to the top—or being appointed at the top—of every bureaucratic organization he was associated with; of producing an exceptional volume of books, articles, and speeches on a wide range of political, legal, and administrative issues; and of not brooking fools—who, for him, were most of the rest of the human race—easily. Interviews with him were likely to be monologues—his monologues—punctuated by the proffering of one or more of his written works to support his points. His meetings with the press frequently produced fireworks, and the press delighted in badgering him to see what sort of quotable response it could elicit. Even telephone conversations could raise his temper. Once, while minister of information and culture, he is said to have become so incensed at the imbecility of his interlocutor at the other end of the telephone line that he pulled the telephone wire out of the wall to cut him off. Putting the receiver back on the hook was not enough; overkill was his problem. He got people's backs up. He inspired uneasiness and even fear as well as respect. His style was doomed to polarize in a Spain that was not in a mood for polarization. Unfortunately for him, his intensity showed through on television and did not make viewing him a comfortable experience. He had a brilliant mind, extraordinary energy, and immense administrative capability. But it was hard for the public to like him and, at a critical juncture, his political judgment proved faulty.

Without Fraga, desultory efforts were made to organize the Center around Areilza, Pio Cabanillas, Joaquín Ruíz Giménez, Fernando Alvarez de Miranda, Joaquín Garrigues Walker, Manuel Cantarero, Francisco Fernández Ordoñez, and others. But no one had the combination of strength of personality, political status, and organizing ability to bring together all the elements involved. Moreover, the Center had its own identity problem. Some centrist politicians called themselves Christian Democrats, some Social Democrats, some Liberals. All tried—probably too hard—to identify with some homologous European or US political group. They should have concentrated more on being Spanish, on responding to Spain's own political realities—as in fact most of them, under Suárez's leadership, eventually did.

Thus, as the elections set for June 15 approached, the Center was fragmented, disorganized, and unready for the fray. In this situation, Fraga's prospects on the right seemed strong, while Felipe González's prospects on the left in fact were strong. In this situation, also, Suárez thought more and more of taking a decisive stand, and the King was urging him to do so. There was much public speculation about what he would do. Some argued that his taking too vigorous a lead from his position as prime minister could place in doubt the legitimacy of these first free elections. Others pointed out that prime ministers all over the world led their parties at election time. At just this point I happened to call on Suárez to take a visiting dignitary to see him. The call was supposed to be simply a brief protocol visit, but Suárez clearly wanted to talk, to express his views on a broad range of matters. He spoke eloquently about the 70 percent of the Spanish populace who were in the Center but who did not have a clear leader. I asked who he thought might provide that leadership. He got a great kick out of this question. He didn't answer it directly, but it was apparent where his thinking was heading. Soon thereafter—following a late April visit to the United States which had nothing to do with his decision—he announced he would head a coalition of Christian Democrats, Liberals, and Social Democrats in the elections under the rubric Union of the Democratic Center (UCD). Areilza thereupon removed himself from the scene, but most others of the Center, except for Ruíz Giménez and Cantarero, fell in with Suárez. Calvo Sotelo was given the last-minute job of knocking heads together among the leaders of the various groups within the UCD over specific candidates for the legislature. In the end, the campaign of the Center, which had been so slow to coalesce, was run primarily on the basis of the attractive Suárez personality, given special cachet by his successful stewardship as prime minister.

A Triumph for the Center—and Suárez. The elections were held on June 15, 1977. It was a "day for the poets," as a leading Spanish political commentator said. The turnout was massive and unmarred by violent incidents. The mood was festive. So thorough were the voting registrars that my diplomatic colleague, the German minister counselor, had a hard time not voting. His name appeared by mistake on the voting register for his ward. He went to the voting table to explain that it would scarcely be appropriate for him to vote. The man watching over the table was puzzled, but argued rather vehemently that since his name was on the register, he really should vote. A Spanish diplomat paid his own way back to Spain all the way from Argentina just to have the experience of voting at home, even though he could have voted by absentee ballot. He was forty-seven years old; having never had the chance to vote, he was not going to miss savoring this opportunity to the fullest. My doorman, whose family was from a country village near Madrid and had also never voted before, came to me a few days before the elections for advice. He was torn between Suárez and Fraga. I told him both were fine men. He voted for Suárez on the premise that he was going to win anyway. Our cook was inclined toward the Communists, but after one of our male servants, who was from Galicia, and his Philippine wife explained that the Communists might take away the apartment she was buying, she also voted for Suárez. So imbued with politics had all levels of Spanish society become that when our butler resigned because of a dispute with our cook, he described the problem to me as "a matter of internal politics," a phrase that never would have occurred to him a year previously.

What sort of person was this young, heretofore relatively unknown man, Suárez, who could take over a government faced with immensely complex issues for which there were really no precedents to provide guidelines; who could lead it surely on a major change in political strategy; who could prepare the nation efficiently and effectively for its first free national elections in forty years; and who could, to boot, take over the Center and persuade the undecided to vote for him? He was, in a phrase, a born politician. He had given evidence of that to those who knew him from his student days in Avila. He was not an outstanding student, but he was effective in personal relations. He had the knack of being sure he was close to people with a future, and of impressing them when they noticed him. He was correct, deferential to those in authority, reliable and serious, but also personable.

After his school days, he became a protégé of a leading politician of the National Movement, Francisco Herrera Tejador. When the latter died in an automobile accident, Suárez moved into Herrera's position as head of the movement. Later, from his position in charge of Spanish national radio and television, he became acquainted and developed a close relationship with Juan Carlos when the latter was still the Prince. Even at that stage, he appeared to have become committed to Juan Carlos. One bit of evidence was a statement he made to me a couple of months before Franco's death to the effect that Franco should resign then in favor of Juan Carlos. This was not the type of thing that the ordinary regime politician was saying even at that late moment.

Suárez was dark, slender, handsome, highly articulate, always immaculately dressed, self-confident, charming, but also careful, hard-working, and, when the time came, decisive. Soon after his assumption of the prime ministership stories began to go around about his fourteen-to-twenty-hour workdays, six to seven days a week; his survival on little food and great quantities of coffee and tobacco; and his commitment to knowing every issue thoroughly and deciding all the important ones himself, in consultation with the King. This latter characteristic led to delays in the address to some issues. He could not personally do everything at once. But when he did come to grips with an issue the results were good.

He was not highly intellectual; in contrast to Areilza and also Fraga, he knew no languages other than Spanish. But he was certainly very intelligent—and extremely pragmatic. In a most un-Spanish way, he believed in compromise. He was spontaneous and very persuasive in intimate dialogue, but serious to the point of somberness in speeches. He was not a committed, back-to-the-wall ideologue. Privately, he was vehemently opposed to communism. But for hard, practical political reasons he could take the step to legalize the Spanish Communist Party. He wanted to win the elections and stay on as prime minister as long as possible, but he was convinced the elections must be spotless and the Socialists must have their fair opportunity. He was a product of the Franco regime, but he conducted the King's opening to the left.

The June 15 elections revealed for the first time for everyone to see the true political map of Spain. They were won, as was to be expected, by the UCD, under the leadership of Suárez, the government's star. The Center obtained 34 percent of the votes and, under the d'Hondt system, further augmented by extra seats for small agricultural provinces, 47 percent of the seats in the Congress of Deputies. The Communists, also as most had expected, revealed their electoral weakness by getting only 9 percent of the vote. The surprises came with the votes for the rightist AP and the leftist PSOE: the former drew only 8 percent of the votes, while the latter, with 29 percent, got more than most expected.* Thus suddenly Spain's political panorama was reduced from hundreds of self-appointed political parties to two with an immediate future, the UCD and the PSOE.†

Thus, too, the King's dramatic gamble of a year earlier paid off. He had gone with an unknown young man to head his government, and that young man had proven himself beyond anything the King could have hoped or anticipated. He had directed an opening to the left, and the voters had shown his political sense to be very much on target. In fact, one might well wonder what the King might have done, or could have done, in the face of still-alive, strong sentiments of the Right and the military, if the PSOE had actually won this election. Neither Spain nor the Socialists themselves, who were short on experienced leadership and long on radical ideological baggage, were ready for that yet; nor were the electors—quite.

---

*The US Embassy's political counselor, Frank McNeil, was, however, exactly on the mark.

†For a fuller description of the Spanish political map, as revealed by June 15, 1977, elections, see David C. Jordan, *Spain, The Monarchy and the Atlantic Community* (Cambridge, Mass. and Washington, D.C.: Institute for Foreign Policy Analysis, 1979), pp. 11–22.

To symbolize further the King's success, his father, Don Juan, who had had his own doubts at the beginning about his son's dedication to democracy, had formally abdicated his rights as the more direct claimant for the throne in a simple family ceremony in Madrid shortly before the elections.

The King's gamble had paid off; June 15 had truly been a day for the poets. But could this sort of atmosphere last in Spain?

COULD EUPHORIA LAST? 5

Could it last?

Spain had risen to a pinnacle of political euphoria on June 15, 1977, as its people went peacefully, orderly, and even joyfully to free legislative elections for the first time in over forty years and returned, in great majority, two presumably—although not yet demonstrably—moderate parties of the Center and Center Left or Left. It accomplished this along an uncharted route, devising the means of travel, and building bridges of compromise as it went. It surprised the skeptics of Europe and elsewhere, and went a long way towards convincing them of its true vocation for democracy. It also gave its own self-confidence a boost. The success of the elections against what to so many, both outside and inside the country, had seemed high odds resulted from the strength of the idea of democracy in the Spain of this period, combined with exceptional leadership by a new generation.

But now, in the next and third phase of the transition, Spain would be faced with problems of governance, institution building, and constitution writing more difficult and challenging, in their ways, than conducting a country used to authoritarian rule to free elections when the great majority of the people so clearly wanted just that. Constitution writing was the top priority for this phase. While the constitution was being drafted, however, the King and the government had also to deal effectively with a deteriorating economy; to make progress on labor policy; to satisfy, on an interim basis at least, persistent demands for regional autonomy; to begin a process of military reorganization; and to move forward with political party building—all this in order to provide programmatic and institutional bases for long-term democratic viability.

Would the idea of democracy and the country's young leadership have the strength and staying power to deal with these difficult problems success-fully? Would the political leaders have the patience and wisdom not to revert from the new-found practices of dialogue and constructive compro-mise to the old habits of destructive confrontation so characteristic of "Celt-Iberians"?* These were the important questions, obscured though they may have been by the euphoria of the moment, as Spain entered the third phase of the transition.

THE ECONOMY: THE MONCLOA PACT

The answer with regard to the economy came first with the naming of the new cabinet. Suárez naturally continued as prime minister. General Gutiérrez Mellado, the King's personal choice for first vice-president for defense affairs, also naturally continued. There was an important change in the other vice-presidency, however. This position had previously been filled by Alfonso Osorio and called vice-president for political affairs, but it had also been the top coordinating spot for economic matters ad refer-endum to Suárez. Now Osorio was made a counselor to the prime minister and Fernando Abril Martorell replaced Osorio as vice-president for political affairs, which was changed to the third vice-presidency. The new vice-presidency was specifically for economic affairs and was filled by Enrique Fuentes Quintana. Fuentes, it will be remembered, was the distinguished economist, respected for his ability by all—Right, Center, and Left—who had turned down a cabinet position in the first Suárez government because he did not think Suárez would have the will or authority to face the coun-try's economic problems squarely. His acceptance of a cabinet position now, and the elevation of that position to the second vice-presidency, sig-naled both a dramatic increase in confidence in Suárez and a decision by the King to give priority attention, at least in principle, to the economy. A similar signal regarding economic policy was transmitted by the naming of Francisco Fernández Ordóñez to the other principal economic position,

---

*In his book *Diary of a Minister of the Monarchy* (Barcelona: Editorial Planeta, 1977) Foreign Minister Areilza describes (p. 59) a difficult session of the cabinet in which his policies were attacked severely, and comments wryly on how easy and natural it would have been to respond heatedly, confronting the opponents in the way that would have been ex-pected of a Celt-Iberian. But oh how effective it was, he continues, simply to turn aside the impassioned criticisms with a soft reply. Suárez's own commitment to avoiding confrontation was demonstrated for all the populace to see on the occasion of a debate in the Cortes over a PSOE attempt to censure the government. The government's minister of the Cortes, Ignacio Camuñas, had risen to reply in vehement, almost violent, terms to the PSOE attack only to have Suárez remonstrate with him in full view of the press immediately afterward, and then remove him from his ministry a few days later.

minister of finance. Fernández Ordóñez had a political base in social democracy for his cabinet position. But he was better known for his competent prior service in subordinate positions up to undersecretary in the Ministry of Finance and, briefly, as president of the principal state holding company, the National Institute of Industries. (He had resigned from the latter post in the autumn of 1974, in protest over the dismissal by Franco of Pio Cabanillas as minister of information).

Historically, the Spanish government's address to economic matters had been uneven. For over twenty years, from the end of the Civil War until 1959, Franco showed little interest in or ability to deal with the economy. Then in 1957 he brought into government a new breed of technocrats, many of them from the Opus Dei, a Catholic religious group whose principal themes are the virtues of hard work and service. Over the years there has been considerable sensationalist speculation over presumed conspiratorial political tendencies of the Opus Dei. This speculation has been fueled by envy of the high positions attained by so many Opus Dei members in both government and business. My belief is that Opus Dei members have done so well primarily because they dedicate their lives so singlemindedly to achievement, not because they have any particular interest in, or bent for, conspiring politically. In any event, the new technocrats, Opus Dei conspirators or not, were extraordinarily successful in contributing, through the policies they instituted, to the economic boom in Spain from 1959 to the early 1970s.

But Prime Minister Arias, perhaps because of a police chief's mind that fed on possibilities of conspiracy, did not like the Opus Dei. Moreover, he is said to have been vastly uninterested in economics. When Arias became prime minister, he quickly removed all Opus Dei members from senior government jobs. From that point until June 1977, political considerations took first place over economic considerations in government decision making. This order of priorities might not have been very serious, since the Spanish economy was going well up to 1974, had it not been for the cumulative effects of the petroleum price increases of 1973. Antonio Barrera Irimo, who was vice-president for economic affairs in the government at the time and had an excellent reputation for financial acumen, made a fundamental misjudgment that Spain would be able to ride out the effects of the petroleum price increase without basic adjustments in its own economic policies. He thought Spain's high reserves at the time (some $6 billion), low level of foreign indebtedness, growth momentum, and extraordinarily low level of unemployment (around 2 percent) would give it the economic cushion it needed; the Spanish people, he thought, had only to wait until the rest of the world, after making adjustments, returned to a prosperity that would spill over to Spain. This spillover, moreover, would curtail such losses as Spain might have incurred in the meantime from having maintained a high growth rate in the face of the burden of increased petroleum prices. He was wrong. The impact of the petroleum prices on both the rest of the world and Spain was deeper and longer lasting than he anticipated. Moreover, Franco governments in their last two years had no taste for demanding sacrifices even when it became clearer that they were necessary. Instead, they were assiduous in providing easy money and encouraging continuing substantial increases in real wages. The economic crisis that was approaching was not yet visible to them; at a time when political ferment was growing, and Franco's physical infirmities becoming increasingly evident, they tended to concentrate on not rocking the political boat rather than on straightening out economic matters.

When Franco died in November 1975, and a new government was formed (but still under Arias's leadership), economic policy did not change fundamentally. True, Arias brought in as minister of finance a dynamic young businessman, Juan Miguel Villar Mir, who might have provided the impetus for a needed policy change. But Villar Mir succeeded in putting his finger on only two elements of the several economic problems facing Spain. At the end of December he made a major speech in which he correctly pointed out that wage increases higher than the country could afford in this period were a major cause of the accelerating inflation, declining foreign exchange reserves, and increasing unemployment. He then devalued the peseta by 10 percent and set out to convince the United States that it should provide a major bailout package.

Villar Mir was technically correct in fingering undue wage increases, and also in devaluing. But that was only part of the story. An overly accommodating monetary policy and continued overreliance on controls also were major contributing factors to Spain's economic problems. Moreover, labor could scarcely be induced to cooperate by the public confrontation that Villar Mir had achieved through his speech. What labor wanted from the government were concessions in terms of rights to organize and function as a collective body. Foreign—or for that matter domestic—sources of capital, public or private, should have had their collective heads examined had they invested heavily on the basis of a partial economic program poorly presented at a moment of political uncertainty. In the event, labor was unresponsive—rebelliously so, indeed, to judge both from its rhetoric and the number of strikes in the first months of 1976. Villar Mir's appeals for foreign assistance were put off by prospective lenders, and the economy, only temporarily assisted by the devaluation, continued to deteriorate. Arias lost his job, not mainly for economic reasons but in circumstances in which his government's economic policy certainly did not help, and Villar Mir departed with him.

Suárez, who succeeded Arias in July 1976, had no experience in national economic issues, and had his hands full with his efforts to establish credibility on the political front. He did try to get Fuentes Quintana to come into his first government, but he did not offer him the top economic job; and Fuentes correctly surmised that Suárez, and perhaps also the country, were not yet ready for decisive economic policy action. I personally believed that the country was ready for economic measures after the referendum of November 1976 in which the people overwhelmingly endorsed the government's program for political reform. But Suárez, and presumably the King, still were not ready. When I made the argument for early strong action on the economic front to one government minister, he countered with the contention—not unfamiliar to our own country of recent times—that unemployment was a greater danger than inflation. He then expressed the view that unemployment had been a major cause of the Civil War in the 1930s. Clearly the psychology of many Spaniards about the political dangers of unemployment relative to those of inflation was quite different from that of the Germans. The Spaniards were conditioned by the effects of worldwide depression on the Spain of the 1930s as manifested in unemployment and political strife. The Germans were and still are conditioned by the political aftermath of the Weimar Republic's hyperinflation of the 1920s.

Stabilization and Consensus. Thus the government continued to temporize until after the elections of June 15, 1977. Then, and only then, was the decision for decisive action made, and the personnel base provided for such action, by the naming of Fuentes Quintana as second vice-president for economic affairs and Fernández Ordóñez as minister of finance. By then, Spain's annual rate of inflation was climbing above 30 percent, foreign debt was piling up, and there was a run on reserves. Something had to be done quickly. Fuentes did it by devaluing by some 25 percent and by announcing a broad stabilization program, but without at that time filling in the details. When the summer weeks passed without any more specifics, observers began to wonder whether this was another false start.

In the autumn, however, Suárez, apparently urged on by Communist Party Secretary General Carrillo, did what was necessary in an unprecedented way. He called the leaders of the major political parties to his residence, the Moncloa Palace, to hammer out a detailed, comprehensive stabilization program with complementary social measures that would have broad political support. The resulting so-called Moncloa Pact included, most notably, provisions that wages would not increase by more than 21 percent over a year's time and that the increase in money supply would be held to 17 percent. Fortunately the budget had not been a great problem;

the Franco governments had been generally conservative in fiscal matters. But greater demands for higher fiscal expenditures doubtless would come later. For the present, stabilization required mainly that spending be held down, not that taxes be increased. That, too, would come later. It was estimated that if the total program succeeded, price increases would be held to 17 percent for the ensuing year, in contrast to some 28 percent for the current year. Actually, the price increase for 1977 would have been well above 30 percent had not the stabilization effort been started in mid-year. The program was presented as achieving continuance of real wage gains by relating prospective wage increases of 21 percent in 1978 to prospective price increases of 17 percent in 1978, rather than to price increases of 28 percent in 1977. Endorsement by the International Monetary Fund was obtained after the fact. Still more important, political support was obtained from all major democratic parties. Some on the Right would have liked a more drastic stabilization effort, while some on the Left would have liked a more liberal program. But the negotiated balance was accepted and supported, and the program in its broad outlines was successful in its first year.

How was it that a basic, classic stabilization effort could be instituted so well by the Spanish government on its own, with no foreign assistance, and so readily achieve the support of all major political factions and even labor? American congressmen passing through Spain asked me this question in amazement—as well they might. The answer lay partly in the excellent professional technicians, headed by Fuentes Quintana, who had been brought into the government in June 1977. It lay also partly in the recognition by all that, in view of the deteriorating situation, something drastic had to be done. But most importantly it was because the parties of the Left—particularly the Communists, but also the Socialists—judged that the economy must be put in shape if the democratic experiment were to prosper. If it did not, then their highly prized opportunities to politick in the open would be gone. They were greatly excited by the new political freedoms and by their chance to participate fully in the political game. They thought continuance of political freedom was their best chance for the future. They did not want to return to jail or exile. They thought the economy could make the difference. It was the strength of the idea of democracy that convinced them as well as others to call on their followers to sacrifice to make the stabilization effort a success. It was as simple, and dramatic, as that.

THE ROLE AND TREATMENT OF LABOR

The economic program could not succeed without the support of labor as well as of the political leaders. Labor's cooperation was achieved partly through political dialogue and persuasion, and partly as the result of the same political reasoning that constrained the political leaders. Communist labor leader Marcelino Camacho presented his position in this regard in an interview with an American correspondent: his party, he said, had backed the Government's economic policy because it believed that the nation's economic crisis was "destroying everything." Without jobs and food, he added, the workers were not going to be able to keep liberty.* Also contributing to labor's cooperation was its knowledge that, given a restrictive monetary policy, undue wage increases could only mean greater unemployment. Government spokesmen carefully and repeatedly spelled this out, with supporting estimates from computers.

Finally, there was the impact of reforms—in the tax field and with regard to labor's organization and rights—that labor had long been seeking. After the June 1977 elections, the second Suárez government, with new Minister of Finance Fernández Ordóñez taking the lead, prepared, presented, and achieved legislative enactment of major tax reform within its first six months—and promised more. With regard to labor organization, a year-and-a-half previously a decision had been made for a plurality of labor unions, on the premise that opting for a single national union would risk Communist control of all labor. Moreover, all trade unions were then permitted to operate in the open. But not until April 1977 was implementing legislation for trade union legalization approved by the Council of Ministers. Other matters always seemed more pressing, and this subject was, in any event, a difficult and thorny one indeed. And not until the autumn of 1977 did the government finally approve a transitional decree for union elections by plant. Following that, during the period from January to April 1978, elections were held that determined formally and freely who should represent labor in each plant.

There was long, sometimes bitter, discussion over the modalities of the elections, with the Socialists accusing the government of favoring election regulations that would help the Communists (the Socialists argued that the government did not want them, its strongest political opposition, to do too well). In fact, the government was interested in seeing so-called independent unions prosper, rather than those identified with either the Communists or the Socialists. However, it did not have the time or the will to do much to forward its interest in this regard.

The end results of these first plant elections found the Communist-affiliated Workers Commissions winning 37 percent of the worker delegates, the Socialist-affiliated General Union of Workers winning roughly 31 percent, and independents the other 32 percent. The Workers Commis-

---

*Wall Street Journal, article by Eric Morgenthaler, 8 June 1978.

sions and the UGT had been expected to come in ahead, but the substantial percentage of workers who voted for affiliation with other unions was encouraging to the government, and to the Union of the Democratic Center. The UCD decided therefore to continue its efforts to build up other unions at that time.

DEMANDS FOR REGIONAL AUTONOMY

The economic crisis and the allied issues of labor policy and institutional demands had the first claims on the government's attention after the June 1977 elections. But simultaneously it had to cope with the insistent demands of several regions, particularly Catalonia and the Basque provinces, for autonomy. The King and Suárez recognized the importance and urgency of this issue by creating a Ministry of Regions and by setting out almost immediately after the election to negotiate interim autonomy arrangements. The government's position was that final arrangements could be negotiated only after the constitution, with definite guidelines, had been approved.

The first autonomy negotiations were with Catalonia. They were greatly facilitated by the availability of a legitimate and easily identified single spokesman for Catalan interests: Josep Taradellas, an imposing, elderly figure of a man, who had spent over thirty years in exile in France. Using a personable former civil governor of Barcelona, Enrique Sánchez Terán, as its liaison man, the government worked out interim arrangements that brought Taradellas back as restored president of the reestablished Generalitat, Catalonia's traditional governing body. One million Catalans demonstrated peacefully in Barcelona for autonomy on September 11, 1977, and on September 29 the Council of Ministers approved reestablishing the Generalitat. Taradellas returned soon thereafter. He and the Catalans were given the symbols and trappings of power in this interim period, but no conclusions were reached as to how many or what powers would be delegated to their regional government after the constitution was approved. This was enough for the Catalans at this stage, and for several other regions suddenly more interested in regional autonomy than before.

It was not enough for the Basques, however, and they lacked a single figurehead to negotiate with the government and bring forceful leadership to their regional council. A preautonomy statute negotiated with the Basques was approved by the Council of Ministers on December 30. But the June elections had shown the Basque Nationalist Party (PNV) to be trailing slightly in the Basque provinces in a close political race with the PSOE. The UCD, which was considerably behind both, nevertheless held the balance of power on the question of which party should hold the presidency of the

Basque regional council set up under the new autonomy act. The government and the UCD opted for the Socialists, presumably on the basis that they had won more votes and were more clearly nonseparatists. Whether this was a good tactic or not is open to question; giving responsibility to the PNV, which was under moderate leadership at that time, might have been the better choice. In any event, the Basques were bitterly disappointed and the situation in the Basque country did not improve. Negotiations with the Basques over the constitution were difficult and contentious; terrorism increased in the Basque country and elsewhere; lack of security discouraged investors, and the economy of the Basque provinces suffered severely. Basque autonomy was clearly one important issue in one important region where the government had not accomplished its purpose of achieving a pacifying compromise. We shall return to this matter in chapter 7.

THE MILITARY: RECALCITRANCE AND REFORM

Relations with the military was another important issue on which all did not go as well as the King and Suárez might have hoped, although some real progress was made on needed basic military reform. The military, it will be remembered, had been deeply disturbed by the legalization of the PCE, and as a result much of its leadership had become anything but enthusiastic about Prime Minister Suárez and first vice-president for defense affairs Gutiérrez Mellado. Two other matters of fundamental concern to high military leaders were the negotiations over regional autonomy and, in the case of the Basque provinces, the associated level of terrorism, which was rising (see also chapter 7). Such terrorism tended to focus on the police but also reached the military directly when General Villaescusa was kidnapped in January 1977 and a general and a colonel were murdered in Madrid in the summer of 1978.

The government's program for reform of military organization and of military personnel policies, while beneficial in the long term, inevitably caused further malaise among the military in the short term. The centerpiece of this reform was the establishment of a Ministry of Defense, with overall coordinating authority; Gutiérrez Mellado assumed another hat to become the first minister of defense. We in the United States know from our own experience after World War II how difficult it is to achieve greater coordination among the military services and what tensions arise in the process of doing so. Spain was going through precisely the same kind of problem. To add to the discomfort caused by this process, military representation in the cabinet was reduced from four—the ministers of the three services and the chief of the high general staff—to one, namely, the newly established and appointed minister of defense. With this action, taken with the naming of a new government after the June 15 elections, the military felt that its voice in government matters was sharply curtailed. Moreover, there was continuing talk about eventual action to lower the retirement age of flag officers from the mid-sixties to perhaps sixty. Few things could be more calculated to focus the minds of the top military officers, most of whom were already in their sixties.

Finally, the conservative military could not help but be uncomfortable with the extraordinary change in Spanish social mores since the death of Franco. Where previously the media had to be the soul of discretion in what they printed, now everything from the most outlandish political ideas to the most erotic photographs appeared. Where before movies and plays were carefully censored to protect the public's morals according to Victorian standards, now anything went.

The disaffection of many of the military with what was going on did not crystallize into any major action, but was evident sporadically in a variety of ways. One bit of evidence was the resignation of Army Chief of Staff Vega in the spring of 1978; there had been months of friction between him and Gutiérrez over lines of authority, and also perhaps over Vega's tendency to cultivate broad political contacts that might imply political ambition on his part. Another, perhaps more serious, bit of evidence was the report that the Foreign Legion leadership, in small meetings that included some politicians of the Right, was actively discussing its distaste with the leadership of the government. Also potentially more serious was the detention of a Civil Guard lieutenant colonel and an Armed Police captain for alleged plotting against the government. Their behavior reflected known unrest in these two important paramilitary public-order forces. Still more evidence of unrest were deprecating remarks made in private about the King by some retired military leaders. One retired general did not hesitate to characterize the King to me as a traitor.

And the disaffection was at times public. In 1977, members of the Civil Guard had held an unprecedented demonstration before the Ministry of Government, in part over bread-and-butter issues but also in part because of dissatisfaction with the degree of support they were getting from the government. Later, a popular Civil Guard leader spoke out, saying the Civil Guard was being asked to undertake public order duties it was unprepared for. He was reassigned, but not otherwise disciplined. Suárez and Gutiérrez Mellado received an extremely cold reaction from families of military leaders at the annual Armed Forces Day parade in June 1978. On this occasion, I saw Suárez and Gutiérrez Mellado ready for a moment to respond to the boos and catcalls that they heard as any Celt-Iberian, or, for that matter, any red-blooded man, might have responded, and then restrain themselves.

Suárez curtly nodded to Gutiérrez Mellado to get into the car and drive off with him. Confrontation was not the name of the game they had played so successfully thus far. It was the name of the game extremists would have liked to provoke them into. Continuing the pattern, at a November 1978 meeting of military officers in Cartagena, a naval captain reportedly harangued against the constitution, and an army general called Gutiérrez Mellado a traitor and a liar and shouted "Viva Franco!"

For a number of reasons, the military was uncomfortable and, to a degree, disaffected. But on the whole it was loyal to the King as supreme commander. The military remained a unifying force at least somewhat above the fray, and was not prepared, at this time, to make any drastic move. It had no single outstanding leader around whom a coup might form. In fact, most of its leadership had reached a time of life when they did not want to be distracted from their comfortable and well-established routine by too much direct involvement in controversial matters. Above all, the military did not have a viable alternative program. Moreover, the people continued to support the government, as was clear from their endorsement of the constitution in the national referendum of December 6, 1978. The military's concerns could, however, give the government pause, and in fact at times did.

POLITICAL PARTY BUILDING

Obviously, there was little time in the second half of 1977 and in 1978 for building party organizations or defining party programs. Yet the parties had to do both in preparation for the national and municipal elections that would follow after approval of the constitution. The results of the June 15, 1977, elections could be interpreted as revealing either primarily an electorate inclined somewhat to the left of center, or one that wanted change without undue disruption. Subsequent opinion polls seemed to support the first of these hypotheses, but without discounting the second. Conceivably, once the desire for political change had been met and the protest against the past had had its day, the pendulum would swing back to the center or to right of center. Only time and future elections would reveal more definitively where the true political balance lay. And that balance would, of course, be affected by intervening events.

The two principal parties of the Left and the party of the Center responded to the electorate's will by moving from their respective prior positions toward the moderate Center Left. The PCE, under Carrillo, continued its decided Eurocommunist line. In response to criticism, particularly from the Socialists, it even went beyond its previous position by renouncing

Lenin and democratic centralism. Felipe González, leader of the PSOE, made a play for the Social Democratic left-of-center vote by suggesting that his party might do well to drop the term "Marxist" from its self-description. The UCD, at the same time, tended to favor Social Democratic positions that represented the left wing of its predominantly center or center-right party.

The movement toward the center left by the leadership of all three of these parties was opposed by important elements of each. There was a goodly number of Communists who didn't agree with giving up Leninism and Socialists Marxism. Neither party was ready to permit itself to be called Social Democratic, although both were acting as though that was what they were. (The posture of the Spanish Communists and Socialists will be discussed further in chapter 6.) The right wing of the UCD was not happy with the preference for Social Democratic positions shown by Adolfo Suárez. Alfonso Osorio gave up his post as a counselor of the prime minister, perhaps in part because he was frustrated by his now minor role, but also in part because he thought business interests were not being given sufficient consideration and that the government was not firm enough on matters of public order. Torcuato Fernández Miranda openly expressed his displeasure with the stance of the government. These were two important names: both had stood high with the King in previous periods. Minister of Justice Landelino Lavilla was said also to favor a more rightist government stance, although he was not prepared to go so far as to leave the government to express his difference. The mayor of Madrid expressed like opinions in a strong speech at the UCD's first national congress in Madrid in October 1978. But Suárez was unperturbed: he was clearly in control of the party, which needed him, and he was determined to respond to what he believed the electorate wanted at this juncture.

With regard to party organization, the PCE and the PSOE entered phase three of the transition after the June 1977 elections in a much better situation than did the UCD. The PCE had been tightly organized under Carrillo's leadership for a long time, while the PSOE, though it had come under Felipe González's leadership relatively recently, had a long tradition (it had, after all, been founded in 1879) and a countrywide organization structure. Moreover, it now broadened its base by bringing in the small but prestigious Popular Socialist Party (PPS) under Tierno Galván.

The UCD, on the other hand, had come under Adolfo Suárez's centralizing leadership only just before the elections; it had no tradition as a party and little organizational structure. It depended on Suárez's charisma, on the fact that so many voters in Spain were in the Center, and on a certain tendency of Spanish voters to prefer the known to the unknown. Its Christian Democratic, Liberal, and Social Democratic components longed to maintain their separate identities, but it was clear they could not if the Center was to prosper—and to govern in a coherent fashion. Other pressing matters tended to preempt Suárez's time, and Center politicians worried over his delays in addressing party matters, but in the end he did turn to party organization. He forced the various component parts of the UCD to renounce their separateness; appointed a prime organizer, first called general coordinator and later secretary general, in the person of a young and able social democrat, Rafael Arias Salgado, who reported directly to him; and, in October 1978, presided over a triumphant party congress attended by such important although rather diverse political personalities as Catholic Party leader Leo Tindemans from Belgium; Conservative Margaret Thatcher from Great Britain; Christian Democrat Mariano Rumor from Italy; Liberal Gaston Thorn from Luxembourg; Social Democrat Fransisco de Sá Carneiro from Portugal; Giscardian Michel Poniatowski from France; and Christian Democrat Eduardo Frei from Chile.

By the end of 1978, then, each of the three principal parties of the Left and Center had positioned itself in the political spectrum and prepared itself organizationally for the political battles to follow approval of the constitution. The fourth principal party, the rightist AP, did not respond to the signs from the election results and the subsequent polls that the electorate leaned to the Center Left or, at the least, wanted substantial, albeit nonradical, change. Fraga did go so far as to take the remarkable step of introducing the leader of the Communist Party, Santiago Carrillo, when the latter spoke at the political discussion club, Siglo XXI. But he seemed stuck for the time being with the other six "magnificent" former Franco ministers, who were more closely identified than he with the authoritarian past—and with the strategy of waiting for the political pendulum to swing back to greater demands for order and authority, if that indeed were in the cards.

CONSTITUTION WRITING

While the economic crisis was being dealt with by a classic stabilization program supported by all major political parties; while the regulations for the first free labor elections in decades were being negotiated and the elections held; while interim autonomy arrangements for regions were being developed, negotiated, and implemented; while structural military reform was being initiated; and while steps were being taken toward clearer definition and better organization of the principal political parties; while all this that was so basic was occurring, the constitution that was to set the legal framework for the future was being drafted in a unique and laborious but politically intelligent manner.

More important than the precise terms of each of the constitution's 169 articles was the way in which the document as a whole was produced, for therein lay the hope that it would last longer than any of its ten predecessors.* Rather than being prepared and presented from above by the government or academe, it was painstakingly negotiated among representatives of the principal political forces. What was sought was consensus. Seven members of the Congress of Deputies, whose parties (according to the calculations of one political observer) represented 85 percent of the electorate, sat as a drafting committee to produce a text for consideration by their parent committee. They took their time, worked carefully, and finished in April 1978. The text had been leaked to the press in an earlier version some months before, giving the drafters the opportunity to test the public's response and to make adjustments. Then followed full committee debate, full debate in the Congress of Deputies, consideration in the Senate, approval by both houses of the legislature, and finally broad approval by the electorate in the referendum.

The AP had serious reservations about the constitution because of the liberal nature of its provisions respecting regional autonomy and issues of religion and education, in particular. Divided within, the AP finally came out in the constitution's favor but left its voters the option of abstaining as an individual act of conscience; significantly, it did not urge them to vote against the constitution. The PNV, which spoke for most Basque nationalists, had serious reservations, feeling that the draft was not specific enough about regional rights, and consequently called for abstention. The cardinal primate of Spain and eight bishops called the draft constitution agnostic, and it was spoken against in their churches. However, the principal church leadership advised Catholics to vote their conscience and implied its support. The far Right and the far Left opposed it. But the UCD and the PSOE, representing by far the largest part of the electorate, endorsed it. Significantly, the PSOE in endorsing the constitution implicitly also endorsed the monarchy, despite its traditional republican stand. The Communists also supported it, as did 88 percent of those who voted in the December 6, 1978, referendum.

On the surface this seemed a solid enough victory for the constitution and the government. *The Economist,* commenting on the referendum, asked in what other Western country would Liberals, Socialists, and Communists have collaborated as closely as they had in Spain in the weeks leading up to the referendum. However, there were shadows on the horizon. More than half of the Basque voters abstained, and nationwide the level of voting was down about 10 percent from the 78 percent who had voted for democracy in

---

*See appendix C for background on Spanish constitutions and a summary of the principal characteristics of the 1978 constitution.

the referendum of December 1976. Euphoria had receded, and the practical difficulty of some problems of governance had become more apparent.

The third phase of the transition was now at an end. It had severely tested the strength and staying power of the idea of democracy; of the new, consensus approach to politics in Spain; and of Spain's young leadership. All three had met the test well, but this time not without warning—particularly in the intractability of the Basque problem and the signs of disaffection in the military and on the Right—of the still difficult path ahead before democracy in Spain could be said truly to be consolidated.

One of the principal sources of military disaffection was the legalization of the PCE. The strength of Spanish socialism, despite years of repression, also worried the military and others on the Spanish Right. The Spanish versions of communism and socialism are considered in greater detail in the next chapter. Following that, in chapter 7, the Basque problem and the general issue of terrorism are discussed more fully.

EUROCOMMUNISM
AND EUROSOCIALISM,
SPANISH STYLE 6

First win the war.
Spanish Communist slogan, ca. 1936*

First the Yugoslavs, then the Chinese and the Albanians, more recently some of the Eastern European countries, and now the Italian, French, and Spanish Eurocommunists have attacked Marxist-Leninist dogma, in one way or another and to one degree or another.

THE SPANISH COMMUNISTS

Santiago Carrillo, secretary general of the relatively small Spanish Communist Party (PCE), which attracted 1.7 million votes out of a total of approximately 18 million in the June 15, 1977 election, has gone the farthest to date.

(1) Carrillo has protested the Soviet invasion of Czechoslovakia in 1968, asserted the right of each communist party to its independent views, and severely criticized Stalinism.

(2) He has rejected—for the industrialized countries—the concept of dictatorship of the proletariat in favor of parliamentary democracy, and praised the King of Spain (whom other Communists might think of principally as

---

*As quoted by Victor Alba, *El Partido Comunista en España* (Barcelona: Editorial Planeta, 1979), Alba describes how the Spanish Communists arrived at the decision in 1936 to work first for victory in the Civil War and concern themselves with the revolution later. He attributes this decision on this occasion to the convenience of the Soviet Union.

a hangover from the feudal past) and Prime Minister Suárez for their contributions to the democratic process in Spain.*

(3) He led a movement, at the national congress of his party in Spain in the spring of 1978, purportedly to do away with democratic centralism and introduce more participation from the base—that is, more real democracy— into party proceedings. In this connection, the international secretary of the PCE's central committee is reported to have said, "We shall no longer identify Leninism as the fountainhead of our inspiration ... we reject every dogmatic reading of Marx." (It is not yet clear how far Carrillo is really prepared to go in giving up democratic centralism, but he made a start in this first move, over considerable opposition. The strong Catalán Communist Party had already in its November 1977 congress reaffirmed its Leninist line, and some of its representatives and a number of others were reluctant to follow Carrillo's new, non-Leninist approach. Carrillo is said to have remarked wryly, when asked about the photographs of Lenin at the PCE congress, that they did seem rather big. But he maneuvered his own way in a congress marked by greater openness than ever before although it was clear that he still dominated it personally.)

(4) He has been equivocal regarding the ownership of means of production. In this connection, he says in the book just cited that the democratic way to socialism—the way he has espoused—assumes the coexistence of public and private forms of property during a long period, and attempts to preserve to the maximum the productive forces and social services already in being, even as it recognizes the role represented in them by private initiative. Foreign capital, under this type of socialism, would be accepted, and capitalist markets would continue to be needed. At the same time, he says, the cardinal objective is to place in the hands of the state and local and regional authorities the decisive levers of the economy, under circumstances in which hegemony would be exercised by a "historic bloc" of labor and cultural forces. His usage doubtless reflects to a considerable degree the influence of the Italian Communist thinker, Antonio Gramsci, who, in the early decades of the twentieth century, stressed the leadership importance of the religious, academic, artistic, and media intellectuals. Carrillo's use of the term "cultural forces" is notably vague in what it encompasses. But, perhaps recognizing the increasingly pluralistic effect

---

*While rejecting the concept of the dictatorship of the proletariat for Western European countries, Carrillo has also maintained, in a work published shortly before the June 1977 elections, that something like it will still be necessary in underdeveloped countries. Moreover, he says the dictatorship of the proletariat was, at an earlier development stage, a historical necessity in the Soviet Union and Eastern Europe, just as revolutionary violence has been even in the bourgeois revolutions. But the dictatorship of the proletariat, he continues, is not the way to establish and consolidate the hegemony of the working forces in the democratic developed capitalist countries. The means of coming to power in these countries is "democracy with all its consequences." See his *Eurocomunismo y Estado* [Eurocommunism and State] (Barcelona: Editorial Critica, 1977).

of industrialization in Europe in this, the second half of the twentieth century, he may go further to include in these forces large segments of the white-collar class.

(5) He has expressed the view that while military blocs should be done away with, United States troops might remain at Spanish bases so long as Soviet troops remained in Eastern Europe. This view was repeated by Manuel Azcárate, one of the leaders of the PCE, in an interview published in 1979. Azcárate said:

> In any case we already have a number of major US bases on our territory, and we have an agreement with the US covering military matters. The Spanish Communist Party does not question either—we accept them. We propose to do nothing to weaken America's strategic position. We do not want to change the existing balance between the United States and the Soviet Union. . . . NATO has created a zone of security in Western Europe which shields those countries which are not members of the alliance. We therefore enjoy indirect protection against Soviet intervention. This is a positive fact about NATO.*

In contrast to the positions taken by Carrillo, the salient points of traditional Marxist-Leninist thought are:

- The inevitable collapse of capitalism and parliamentary democracy because of internal contradictions deriving from, first, the exploitation of labor, and then, overinvestment, overproduction, overconcentration, and increasingly severe business crises.
- Provision of markets for capitalist production as the primary purpose of colonies. Their exploitation could postpone but not prevent the inevitable collapse of capitalism.
- The temporary replacement of capitalism and of parliamentary democracy by a socialist society in which all means of production are socialized and there is a dictatorship of the proletariat. This will be achieved through the revolutionary action of a small, centralized party within which tight discipline is maintained through democratic centralism.
- Eventual withering away of classes and of the state, and thus achievement of communism.
- And homage to the Soviet Union as the original pioneer and leader of the process.

Is Carillo a Social Democrat? When Kenneth Clark, in his masterwork on art and music, *Civilization,* comes to opera, in which the hero of the piece sings unintelligible stanzas in a series of improbable situations, he expresses his perplexity at this art form with the phrase "What on earth is going on here?" We may well ask the same question of all Eurocommunists,

---

Encounter, March 1979, p. 22 (interview with George Urban).

and particularly of Santiago Carrillo. If a Communist gives up the dictatorship of the proletariat and democratic centralism, embraces parliamentary democracy and even a monarchy, admits the virtues of a mixed economy, criticizes the external aggressiveness and internal repressiveness of the Soviet Union, and condones the presence of American armed forces in Spain, is he still a Communist or is he now a Social Democrat?

Santiago Carrillo insists he is not a Social Democrat. He says in *Eurocomunismo y Estado* that the Eurocommunists propose to transform capitalist society, not to administer it. He continues that they will not abandon the revolutionary ideas of Marxism, the notion of the class struggle, historical materialism and dialectical materialism, or the concept of a worldwide reach that will end imperialism. Moreover, he points out that he does not reject the taking of power in a revolutionary manner if the dominant classes close the democratic paths and if the situation is propitious to the revolutionary way.

Yet in the same work he also affirms the following (in rough summary):

> The industrialized democracies are ripe for the achievement of socialism through pluralistic, parliamentary democracy. "Material commotions" in economic production, with extraordinary changes in social and political relationships, makes this so. These commotions and changes are (1) progress in production, thanks to technology; (2) broad extension of education; (3) the undermining of private initiative through its inability to cope with the needs of large-scale, high-technology industry without state subvention; (4) the tendency of the large economies to be dominated by a few large monopolies; (5) the assumption by the state of broad social functions; (6) increases in differences between the oligopolistic minority that controls the state and the bulk of the society (he calls this the "proletarization" of the masses, as they resist concentration of capital and control); and (7) the independence of the former colonies.
>
> The "ideological apparatuses" of the state—the church, the family, the educational system, the political parties, the courts, the media—are all now divided and potentially opposed to a state controlled by monopolies. The military is also beginning to question the status quo and, in some countries, is beginning to be democratized. The Communist Party must work to broaden its base in society and gain control of the ideological apparatuses. It should win over the military by being responsive to its needs. It should attempt to achieve hegemony over the state for the proletariat and the forces of culture through democratic means, not through violence or coups, and through demonstrated independence from the Soviet Union. Violence or attempted military coups have been successful where the military has been demoralized by losses in war. But they would normally be too dangerous in the advanced industrialized countries, if only because of the risk of intervention by the

Great Powers, perhaps even at the nuclear level. At the same time, the political position of the proletariat and of the forces of culture is very much better either than it was in the past in the now-developed countries, or than it is now in developing countries, because of the increase in number of both elements with industrialization, and because of the greater sympathy by the ideological apparatuses for their cause.

Under the new circumstances the Communists will not be the only, or perhaps even the dominant, representatives of the working class and the forces of culture. They will be the vanguard; their mission is simply to contribute to the achievement of hegemony in the state by the proletariat and the forces of culture, who will then represent all the people. This could be achieved through a confederation of like-minded political parties or groups. *The Communists and the Social Democrats should, in time, converge.* The Communists must become less sectarian, more accustomed to speaking in the name of the majority of the society. Universal suffrage is not the only road to power, but in the Europe of today the socialist forces can, through universal suffrage, first enter government and then, if they can maintain the confidence of the people as expressed in periodic elections, gain and maintain hegemony. In a real democracy, the masses must, however, be in a position to express themselves at all times, not just through elections.

But are Santiago Carrillo's strongly expressed beliefs, as here summarized, based on real conviction, or has he adopted them for purely tactical purposes? We cannot be sure. But let us consider briefly Carrillo's own history and that of the PCE, and then apply reason to this central question. Carrillo was originally a leader of the Spanish Socialist (PSOE) youth. The PSOE youth and the Communist (PCE) youth merged in April 1936. At about that time young Carrillo became a PCE member. The PCE, with strong competition for the Left from the PSOE and the Anarchists, had never been very large or successful. But during the Civil War period it became more successful because of disciplined organization, because it was the channel for Soviet supplies, and because it began a policy of courting the bourgeoisie through protestations of moderation in order to expand its membership and support. Its theme was win the war first and have revolution later.

Carrillo was almost expelled from the PCE in 1955 and 1956 because he argued, against the views of the PCE's old guard, that Spain's entry into the United Nations was a logical extension of the theory of coexistence and thus a good thing. His position soon gained support, however, in considerable part because of the effect on the PCE of Khrushchev's denunciation of Stalin at the twentieth CPSU congress. Moreover, Carrillo pressed the idea at about that time that a series of strikes in Spain, the first serious ones since the Civil War, signaled that the fall of Franco was at hand. He was wrong, but his activism in promoting a subsequent general strike helped strengthen his role in the PCE. In 1960 he became its secretary general. By 1968 he was sufficiently disillusioned with events in the Soviet Union to denounce strongly the Soviet invasion of Czechoslovakia.

It would seem entirely logical that Santiago Carrillo should be a true nationalist whose bravado is reinforced by two fortunate advantages: geographic distance from the raw power of the Soviet Union, and the existence of NATO. Both give him the luxury of asserting his independence from the Soviet Union with considerable impunity. His relatively recent rediscovery of his nationalism (it was not so apparent during the Civil War or the Soviet invasion of Hungary) may be the result not only of the 1968 Soviet invasion of Czechoslovakia, which on the surface would seem to have been a watershed experience for him, but also of a growing disenchantment with the way the Soviet system has functioned in comparison with the mixed-economy systems of Western Europe. Why Carrillo reacted so strongly to the invasion of Czechoslovakia after not having done so to the invasion of Hungary requires explanation, part of which may lie in the revelations, from 1956 onwards, of the political excesses and economic failures of Stalinism. It is also likely, however, that he has been impressed by the successes of the working class and the increased importance of the professional and service sectors of society in systems governed by social democratic governments.

Carrillo criticizes Stalinism severely. He calls it "totalitarian socialism," with serious perversions through police repression, a large military establishment, and bureaucratic control. He comments: "If all states are instruments of the domination of one class over another and in the USSR there are no antagonistic classes . . . then who does the state in the USSR need to dominate? The October Revolution has produced a state that . . . is not yet an authentic workers democracy."* He then speculates that perhaps, at the stage in which the USSR was at the time of the 1918 Revolution, a repressive dictatorship was needed to achieve the "original accumulation of capital" required for modern industry. The problem with this speculation is that if it is valid, the bureaucratic, dictatorial state in the Soviet Union, though a tool for achieving the same economic progress that the capitalistic states have achieved, still continues to be a serious obstacle to democracy. Perhaps it is thus an intermediary phase, he muses. But why it was necessary, and preferable to capitalism, he does not say; indeed, he remarks on how slowly economic and social transformation has gone in the Soviet Union. Nor does he comment on how the Soviet Union will be able to move from a bureaucratic to a democratic workers' state, except to note that the flow of credits

---

*Eurocomunismo y Estado, p. 201.

and technology from the West could have some influence.

While taking Stalinism so severely to task, Carrillo is, as we have seen, highly positive about the extraordinary economic progress made in the industrialized democracies with the use of advanced technology, and about the accompanying social advances in education and other areas. Moreover, as we have also noted, he sees the state (not the capitalists) as almost inevitably having a dominant role in these societies because of the increased dependence of the capitalists on it. Even so, Carrillo's embracing of parliamentary democracy as the appropriate route to power—aside from some possible exceptions—for the communist parties of Western Europe is also clearly logical from a tactical point of view. In fact, it is almost imposed upon him because there is today no promising alternative to this route in Western Europe. One can assume he does not want to take the risks Salvador Allende took in Chile, nor the position that failed for Alvaro Cunhal in Portugal, by attempting to move too far too fast against the Right. Thus the question of whether his motives are principally tactical or not is still not adequately answered.

Carrillo the Cryptic. This brings us to what may be the real crux of the matter. What kind of society does Carrillo really envisage over the longer term, and what are the implications of that kind of society? Stated more precisely, how convinced is he now that the ultimate communist goal of socialization of all means of production must be achieved, given his second thoughts about communism since Stalin's death? If, in effect, he still wants to achieve a society in which all, or virtually all, means of production are in the hands of the government, then his brand of Eurocommunism would not pass the ultimate test of orderly alternation in power with other political parties according to the electorate's will. It would not pass this test for three reasons, the most basic of which is simply that government ownership and management of all means of production, even if, in communist jargon, in the name of the people, requires such centralization of authority as to be impossible without totalitarianism. The second, allied, reason is that this traditional brand of communism could not gain and then retain power without resort to severely repressive measures, as the public became fully aware of its intentions and their consequences. This was the problem that eventually faced Allende in Chile; even after gaining power by democratic means, Allende so alienated the power centers of the polity by his radical, inefficient, and disruptive economic program that he could not have retained power without resort to force. The third reason is that even if Carrillo moved slowly enough once in power to avoid being thrown out before he was voted out, those of his policies that would radically transform the society would tend to be reversed by the government that replaced him because of their inherent inefficiency and their requirements for all-encompassing centralized control.

The same conclusions may be reached if one assumes that Carrillo now wants to achieve a Yugoslav-style self-management society. That would also be too disruptive, too dependent on command from the center, and too inefficient by comparison with a mixed-economy approach to lend itself to a periodic acceptance and rejection pattern through alternation of political parties.

In both cases that have been postulated, Carrillo's central political problem would be the implicit assumption of the achievability of a classless or one-class society of social and political robots, in which all would be in agreement with either centralized bureaucratic control of all economic activity or worker control of all economic activity. Since no such society would or could exist democratically, it could be achieved only by force and, eventually, by totalitarianism.

The touchstone for judging Carrillo's true intent—and, likewise, the true intent of other Eurocommunists—must then be the acceptance of pluralism, not only politically but also socially and economically, in all societies that may evolve in the future. If, for instance, Carrillo were to aim ultimately for only a moderate degree of worker self-management, or industrial democracy, without going the whole hog, his statements of democratic intent would be more credible. Comanagement after all, is already being experimented with to one degree or another in several Western European countries under democracy. Moreover, it may be recalled that Western European democracies have similarly experimented with degrees of nationalization under democracy. It is conceivable that the advance of comanagement, which can have a variety of forms, and which potentially could increase the workers' sense of responsibility for both macro- and microeconomic events, and thus improve the functioning of mixed economies, would be enough to satisfy Carrillo in his lifetime. It is conceivable also that this, together with other social and economic advances already achieved or on the way in advanced industrialized democracies, would be all the restructuring or reforming of society that Carrillo would really wish to see over the long term. Conceivable, but not even to be taken as a serious possibility unless and until he himself becomes much more specific on this issue than he has been thus far. And he is unlikely to become specific, because in so doing he would be saying, with no defense, that he definitely is a Social Democrat, not a Communist.

It is noteworthy that in *"Eurocomunismo" y Estado*, he says very little that is helpful in adjudicating these vital matters. He says that the democratic road to socialism presupposes the coexistence of public and private forms of ownership, but he qualifies this statement by limiting it to a "presocialist" phase. He tries to distinguish Eurocommunism from social democracy by saying that Eurocommunism would transform capitalism, not administer it, but he does not explain what that means. He talks of replacing the hegemony that a few monopolists exercise over the state with a hegemony of the working and cultural forces, which he apparently assumes would eventually encompass most of the society, and he then says that the Communists do not assume they will be the only or even the dominant political party representing these forces. But he does not go on to say what the program of the newly hegemonic working and cultural forces would be.

Thus one is left quite unclear regarding the type of society Carrillo is really aiming at, and, from his tactical point of view, with good reason. If he were to say specifically that he continues to believe in the end of private ownership and of private control of the means of production, he would reveal clearly for all to see that his protestations of political moderation are unrealizable and a sham. If, on the other hand, he were to say that he now believes in a mixed economy forever, that statement, along with the political positions he has taken, would mark him ideologically as an unmistakable Social Democrat. Therefore he is, and must be, vague. On the one hand he seems very impressed by the achievements of modern capitalism and willing to live with a continuation of mixed economies for an indefinite period. On the other hand, he talks of transformation. Moreover, while embracing parliamentary democracy, he also says there might be circumstances, even in the advanced democracies, in which violent revolution would be necessary and advisable.

Given this fundamental lack of clarity of commitment to economic and social as well as political pluralism, and given the only logical explanation for his fuzziness on this issue, why should one take risks on the assumption of Carrillo's commitment to what is really social democracy? The answer is that there is no sound reason why one should. This question becomes even sharper when one remembers that so many in the PCE are not comfortable with Carrillo's apparent moderation, and that there is at least one other party in Spain, namely the PSOE, that is more credibly social democratic. However, as we shall see, even the PSOE's social democratic credentials are not impeccable.

SPANISH SOCIALISM

The Western European version of socialism is radically different from the Marxist-Leninist version. It completely rejects totalitarian ideas and regimes, and with them the concepts of dictatorship of the proletariat and democratic centralism. In their place, it maintains that socialism as a social and economic ideal is inseparable from the idea of democracy; it completely accepts parliament, not revolution, as the means to power; and it also accepts the transformation of the laboring-class socialist parties of the past to broader-based people's parties seeking the general welfare. It is thus generically social democratic. It has given up the idea of state ownership as a "first principle" of socialism and substitutes public control of enterprise and planning as the best means of achieving a fair distribution of wealth. It concentrates on control, rather than ownership, of industry; on social equality, including, especially, equal education for all; and on citizen participation in government, especially at the work place. Involvement of workers in company management—that is, "industrial democracy"—is now a principal objective of many Western European socialist parties. A major precursor of current social democratic ideas was Eduard Bernstein (1850–1932), who believed, in contrast to Lenin, that the working class could win peacefully within a gradually reforming capitalist system. A crossroads in the Western European interpretation and practice of socialism was the West German Bad Godesburg Declaration in 1959, which contained no reference to Marx; it stated that private ownership of the means of production was entitled to protection and promotion so long as it did not hinder the construction of an equitable social order. Thus Marxian socialism had its Eurosocialism long before Marxist-Leninist communism had its Eurocommunism.

The Spanish Socialists' problem with regard to socialism Western European style is the opposite of the Spanish Communists' problem with regard to communism Eastern European style. Whereas Santiago Carrillo and his followers sound and act altogether too much like Social Democrats for the taste of the orthodox Communists of the East, the Socialist Workers Party (PSOE) of Spain had, from the Civil War until recently at least, sounded altogether too Marxist to be social democratic. But Felipe González, the PSOE's secretary general, perhaps out of personal conviction and certainly in careful calculation of where he thinks the votes are in the Spain of today, is trying to change that.

Is Felipe González a Marxist? The PSOE, as its name so clearly suggests, has traditionally been a working-class party. It was the principal party of the Spanish Left before and during the Civil War. From its founding in 1879 until the 1920s it was democratic, moderate, and pluralistic. Its leading figure in this period was Pablo Iglesias (1850–1925). But during the Civil War, under the influence of Francisco Largo Caballero, it adopted Marxist positions. After the war it was the subject of harsh repression; its leadership was jailed or exiled and lost effectiveness. Splinter groups grew up in Spain. Finally, at the party's congress in October 1972, a group of young turks gained control; they were headed by Felipe González, a labor lawyer from Seville who was still only thirty. In 1973 the Socialist International gave its blessing to these young leaders.

In its December 1976 congress the PSOE formally defined itself as Marxist. A leading thinker of the small Popular Socialist Party (PSP) that merged with the PSOE after the 1977 elections argued to me in one conversation in early 1978 that the PSOE must remain clearly identified as working class and Marxist if it was not to lose too many votes to the Communists. At the same time, however, this Socialist thinker maintained, contradictorily, that the PSOE must attract more professional-class and white-collar voters.

Therein lies the dilemma that then faced Felipe González. Which of these two mutually contradictory routes, so long debated within the party, should he take? Should he try mainly to gain votes in the moderate Center Left, assuming that this was where the real future was, or should he try mainly to keep the loyalty of his presumed radical base? Indeed, was his radical base really very broad, even among the workers? He chose in 1978 to concentrate more on attracting a broader range of voters from the Center Left than on retaining the allegiance of the radical leftist members of his party. He foreshadowed this position by saying publicly in the spring of 1978 that he thought the PSOE should drop the term "Marxist" from its self-description. Subsequently, in an interview with the conservative newspaper *ABC* in October 1978, he expressed himself most clearly as favoring a social democratic approach:

> The PSOE is capable of integrating within it people who feel themselves to be non-Leninist Marxists. Those who consider themselves to be Leninists and are in the PSOE either are infiltrators or are in the wrong home. The PSOE also has a place for those who feel that they are social democrats and do not identify themselves with Marxism, just as it does for those with humanist positions, whether Christians or otherwise . . . .

González went on to say that he did not define himself as a Marxist because that would be too narrow and would not take into account other contributions that came after Marx. He then was quoted as saying succinctly and categorically that social democracy's place was in the PSOE, not in the governing Union of the Democratic Center (UCD).

This was against a backdrop of PSOE rhetoric that had been long on dedication to structural reform, and that had frequently stated the goal of worker self-management as though the PSOE would have Spain become the Yugoslavia of tomorrow tonight. However, the president of the PSOE, Ramón Rubial, a septuagenarian worker-philosopher from the Basque country in the Eric Hoffer mold, said to me when I first saw him in 1977 that this was a very long-term goal. And González himself had gone out of his way to try to quiet the fears of private-sector investors, both in Spain and (during a visit in November 1977) in the United States, with moderate statements regarding nationalizations in Spain. On this score, the PSP thinker referred to above expressed the view to me—rather surprisingly in light of his other statements that I have described—that were the PSOE to come to power, its program would be more like Sweden's than Yugoslavia's.

Under González's leadership the PSOE tried to establish an image of moderate opposition to the UCD, while cooperating on essential programs such as the economic stabilization effort and the drafting of the constitution. Its strongest barbs were for the Communists. It pointed to the PCE's history of democratic centralism. González was reported in the press as saying a communist party is a communist party, and if it changes it should no longer call itself communist. He is also quoted as saying the PSOE would have problems working in coalition with the PCE because, among other things, it would be difficult to imagine the Communists contributing to the construction of a social democracy in which liberties prospered.

During the same period, the PSOE's leaders from time to time indicated they might be prepared to enter into a coalition government with the UCD. The reason for this may have been in part their knowledge that they were painfully short of top-quality administrators with management experience. They considered themselves a legitimate alternative to the UCD as the governing party. But they knew they were not yet well prepared, and they would not have minded the opportunity to have more experience before having the ultimate responsibility. They were young, they assumed they had a long future, and they did not want to spoil that future by moving too fast.

The PSOE top leadership was divided in its ideological orientation. González talked like a Social Democrat although he did not put himself in that category. Alfonso Guerra, usually spoken of as his immediate deputy, was a vehement Marxist. Enrique Múgica, considered next in line, freely called himself a Social Democrat. Thus the socialist spectrum was bracketed, but the ideological, and also pragmatic, position of the party was uncertain.

The Socialists and the King. The PSOE is, of course, traditionally republican. As a republican, Felipe González does not like to admit that King Juan Carlos is any different from other Spaniards. According to one story, he was fond of saying, when describing the King, that Juan Carlos was simply another young Spaniard who happened to be a tall, blond, blue-eyed man who liked sports. The story continues that Juan Carlos found this rather amusing, and that Felipe had to change his tune somewhat after Juan Carlos came up to him at a reception and said, "Felipe, look me in the eyes. What color are they?" Felipe had to confess they were brown.

The PSOE maintained its republican position throughout the drafting of the constitution, but in the end did not make a major issue of the inclusion in it of provisions for the continuation of the monarchy. Its leaders fully recognized the contribution that King Juan Carlos had made to the transition to democracy. That contribution was very important to them. They also recognized Juan Carlos's popularity with much of the populace. An anecdote will illustrate. In the summer of 1978, a group of congressmen visited Madrid and I arranged for them to have lunch and an extended post-luncheon conversation at my residence with some of the principal Socialist leaders, including Enrique Múgica. The conversation tended to concentrate on socialist themes and on NATO. Toward its end, one of the Republican members of the congressional group, no doubt somewhat bored, thought he would add a little humor to the afternoon that had been dominated thus far all too much by his Democratic colleagues and the Socialists. He said, "Mr. Múgica, are there any Republicans in Spain?" He no doubt did not realize that Múgica would think in terms of generic, antimonarchical republicans, with a small "r," rather than US Republicans with a capital "R." Múgica thought for a moment and then replied wryly, "Mr. Congressman, everybody in Spain is a republican. The only trouble is that everybody also likes Juan Carlos."

SOME CONCLUSIONS

The current leaders of both the Spanish Communist Party and the Spanish Socialist Workers Party have moved toward moderate left or center-left, social democratic positions. They have done so in response to their conviction that their best chances for the future lie with the success of Spain's democratic experiment, in which they are free to participate fully in the political competition for votes. They are also convinced that the biggest bloc of voters is in the Center Left.

The PCE has been at a distinct disadvantage in competition with the PSOE, both because it began with many fewer voters, and because its own record and that of its sister parties elsewhere make its professions of democratic vocation much less credible than the PSOE's. Voters could, and certainly should, readily and legitimately ask why they should take the risk of voting for the PCE, despite its seeming moderation on political issues, as long as there is at least one other moderate option, the PSOE, with a long history of democratic practice, despite its ideological ambiguity.

The prospects for the PSOE to maintain its long lead over the PCE as prime representative of the Spanish Left will probably depend mainly on how good its leadership is in convincing the Spanish people that it is a viable moderate alternative to the UCD. For it to do this, most of its principal leadership must accept social democracy, but that this has been a difficult step for a number of them to take became only too clear in the first half of 1979.

Electorates tend to want at least two alternatives from which to choose. In Italy, because the Socialists did not provide a credible alternative to the Christian Democrats, the electorate turned more to the Communists. In Spain, if the Socialists could achieve credibility as an alternative, the Communists would be unlikely to benefit. If the Socialists fail, however, then the Communists may in time gain substantially. Spanish communism under Carrillo has been extraordinarily adept at creating an attractive image of moderation and responsibility, despite many good reasons for not trusting this imagery over the long term. Unless the PSOE defines itself more clearly as social democratic, the situation of the Spanish Left could evolve along French lines, at the least, with the Socialists divided and the Communists profiting thereby.

BASQUE AUTONOMY AND THE DILEMMAS TERRORISM SPAWNS 7

Early on the morning of December 20, 1973, Admiral Carrero Blanco, prime minister of Spain, came out of the Jesuit Church across from the American Embassy in the heart of Madrid; he had just been to mass. He got into his chauffeur-driven car. The chauffeur followed his usual morning route exactly at the usual times—left at the first corner, left at the next corner, and—then—an extraordinary explosion! It ripped a huge hole in the street, blowing car and occupants five stories in the air. Wreckage and bodies came down in the church patio. Suddenly, Franco's first prime minister was no more; and terrorists, presumed to be of the Basque separatist organization, Basque Homeland and Liberty (ETA), had demonstrated more dramatically than ever before their capacity to do mischief or, according to one's point of view, to take direct, positive action to change the atrophied, unjust Franco system of government.

Generalísimo Franco's reaction was, on the surface, what one might have expected. He selected as Carrero Blanco's replacement a man with a strong police background, Carlos Arias Navarro, popular ex-mayor of Madrid, but also ex-director general of security, and then minister of government. Presumably Franco thought Arias was the sort of man to deal with a quite evident security problem. Arias, however, reacted not as expected, especially by Franco. Within two months the new prime minister made the now well-known Spirit of February 12 speech, in which he called for political liberalization. It could thus be argued that the terrorists had achieved an important purpose. Whether or not that purpose—political liberalization—*was* their purpose is, however, a matter of considerable question.

TERRORISM AND PUBLIC ORDER

The spectacular assassination of Carrero Blanco occurred in Madrid, and other such incidents were staged by other terrorist groups in Madrid and elsewhere outside the Basque country. But it was in the Basque provinces where tension was highest. There, in addition to other acts of violence, the public-order forces—the Civil Guard and the Armed Police—were continually subjected to harassment and assassination by the ETA and reacted in kind against terrorists or demonstrators. The government's response to continuing terrorism was understandably punitive. It could not lightly countenance the level of terrorism that existed, including the killing of public officials. In the spring of 1974 it went through with the execution of an anarchist in Barcelona accused of complicity in the assassination of a policeman. And at the end of September 1975 it proceeded with the execution of five terrorists convicted in military court of having been responsible for blood crimes.

Many observers, however, including a number of Western European governments, interpreted the terrorism in Spain as a justifiable reaction to authoritarianism, and the executions as further acts of political repression on the part of a dictator. There were protest demonstrations in many European cities. Differences of viewpoint over the executions were graphically in evidence at an annual reception held by Franco on October 1, 1975, less than two months before his death, for major government and private-sector leaders and the diplomatic corps. In protest over the executions, not one Western European diplomat went to the reception. Moreover, as the Spanish dignitaries filed past Franco and, beside him, Prince Juan Carlos, one noted now and again a second of hesitation. To whom to bow? How deeply? Or at all?

I was US chargé d'affaires at the time. I told my ambassador, who was home in the United States, of the issue being discussed within the diplomatic corps with regard to attendance or nonattendance at the reception and suggested it might be just as well if he did not hurry back to be present for this occasion. For my part, I had no doubt that, as chargé, I ought to attend, since we had close relations with the Franco regime for national security reasons. True, we were attempting to hedge our bets for the future by establishing contacts with potential future leaders. But I did not think there was a good reason for us to make a diplomatic scene on behalf of the terrorists. I was not convinced they were necessarily legitimate promoters of the cause of liberty—a judgment that would seem to have been borne out by subsequent experience. I did not ask the Department of State for instructions as to whether I should attend the reception; I was quite sure I knew the answer. I simply told my ambassador that I would of course plan to go, and went. As it turned out, I was relatively alone as a diplomat from an industrialized democracy among Third World and Eastern European diplomats, none of whom seemed to have any of the concern over the matter that kept the Western Europeans away. A few days later a number of ambassadors who had been conveniently out of town returned, and this little diplomatic minuet passed into history, leaving behind simply two interesting questions: how legitimate were the terrorists as defenders of liberty, and what level of diplomatic support did they really merit.

During 1976 and 1977 the level of killing by both the ETA and the police in the Basque country declined as the King's government, after Franco's death, issued successively more liberal amnesties for political prisoners and began the process of democratization. It even appears that there may have been a tacit truce between the government and the ETA for a period of time. After the June 15, 1977, legislative elections and the final amnesty that followed shortly and resulted in the release from jail of virtually all remaining "political" prisoners, including those accused of murder of public officials, there would seem to have been no further justification for terrorism—that is, if its only cause had been political repression at the national level. But that was not its only or, indeed, its primary cause.

The Issue of Basque Autonomy. The Basque demand for autonomy—independence even—was more fundamental. This cause was strong in the minds of many of the people of the Basque provinces, and was intermixed with the idea of ending Francoist authoritarianism and achieving democratic and civil liberties.

The desire for a degree of Basque autonomy had deep roots. Historically, the Basque provinces in northern Spain—Guipuzcoa, Vizcaya, and Alava—had enjoyed broad self-government for a long period of time, while officially pledging allegiance to the Spanish crown. Navarra, with a considerable Basque population, had formerly been an independent kingdom. In the eleventh century the local rights and privileges of Basque provinces and townships were codified into *fueros* (exemptions), under which the King of Spain ruled by consent rather than right. The *fueros* remained in force, or essentially so, until the reign of Carlos III (1759–1788). Throughout the early nineteenth century they were, however, a major issue. Meanwhile, the three neighboring French Basque provinces were subjugated by the central French government at the end of the eighteenth century, after the French Revolution. At the conclusion of the second Carlist war in Spain (1872–1876), the Spanish Basques, having been on the losing side, were stripped of most of their traditional liberties, but were left with some degree of fiscal and administrative autonomy. The new arrangements were known as the *conciertos económicos* (economic agreements).

From this time until near the end of the nineteenth century the spirit of Basque autonomy seemed to wane, the speaking of the Basque language declined, and there was greater continuous assimilation of the population of the Basque provinces into the Spanish culture. But the desire for greater autonomy remained very much alive and in 1893 found a leader in Sabino de Arana Goiri, the son of a Basque industrialist, who launched the modern Basque nationalist movement by publishing a tract advocating Basque nationalism and independence and by forming the Basque Nationalist Party (PNV). He coined the term Euskadi to refer to the Basque nation, argued against intermarriage with non-Basques, promoted the study of the Basque language, and advocated the expulsion of non-Basques from the Basque provinces.

In the last respect at least, he was singularly unsuccessful. Instead, the number of non-Basques in the Basque provinces increased as iron mining advanced the industrialization of the area and employment opportunities multiplied, attracting a steady stream of immigrants from poorer regions of Spain. According to a recently published study by Pedro de Yrizas, only some 455 thousand of the 2.3 million population of the four Basque provinces now actually speak Basque (*Euskera*). This figure of some 20 percent contrasts with one of some 50 percent at the time of the Civil War. Stanley Payne states that only about 12 percent of the Basque population is able to write Basque.*

Nevertheless the Basque autonomy movement prospered. The Basques are strongly independent by nature, and their culture differs from that of other Spaniards. The Basque language is not at all like Spanish. In fact, it is non-Latin. Some say it has roots in Georgia in the Soviet Union, others that it is related to Hungarian, which came originally from the Urals. The Basques were traditionally small farmers, or fishermen and whalers, then miners, then industrialists and financiers—all callings that foster strength, independence, and risk taking. Moreover, second-generation immigrants to the Basque provinces have often identified themselves with Basque nationalism.

During the Civil War an autonomous regional Basque government was established for a short period of time. With the victory of the Franco forces, the Spanish government entered into a program of reprisals against Basque nationalists, numbers of whom were shot or imprisoned. The government also abrogated the *conciertos económicos* for Vizcaya and Guipuzcoa and launched a program of forced assimilation, prohibiting all manifestations of Basque culture and identity. But the repressiveness of the Franco government only whetted the Basques' appetite for autonomy. The lack of confidence among the populace of the Basque provinces in the central government in Madrid, and the hatred of public-order forces directed from Madrid, increased in the Franco period. And Basque nationalist politicians pressed

---

*Stanley G. Payne, *Basque Nationalism* (Reno: University of Nevada Press, 1975).

hard again for autonomy, or independence, after Franco's death.

Decentralization versus Independence. The Suárez government attempted to respond to the deep feeling for autonomy among the Basques by negotiating an interim autonomy agreement with them, as it did with the Catalans and others. It also tried to educate the police and Civil Guard to be gentler in their handling of public-order problems in the Basque country. (This was not easy in view of their long years of training to be tough on the Basques and the continuing general nastiness and deliberate provocativeness of the terrorists.) The Basques accepted the interim autonomy statute strictly for what it was, namely, an interim measure pending further negotiations. They attempted to achieve more during the drafting and approval of the constitution, and gained sufficient concessions to cause concern within the rightist Popular Alliance Party (AP) and the military, but not sufficient to satisfy their own aspirations. The two principal issues under debate in the constitution-drafting period were whether certain responsibilities would be transferred, instead of being delegated, from the central government to the eventual Basque government; and whether certain—the Basques would say extensive—liberties eventually to be restored to the Basques would be under a constitution governing all Spaniards or, instead, established without reference to the constitution. The Basque negotiators attempted to achieve a return to a special situation in which Basque allegiance to Spain could be expressed through a pledge of allegiance to the King or, in other words, through Basque consent rather than royal right. These were rather basic issues conceptually—issues that separated the idea of autonomy from that of almost complete independence. In the end the constitution resolved the issue as follows: (1) it provided for linguistic pluralism but gave preeminent status to Castilian over "other Spanish languages"; (2) it permitted use of regional flags provided they were flown beside Spanish flags; (3) it stated that the traditional rights of the "foral territories" (that is, areas with *fueros*) would be respected, but added that this would be done within the framework of the constitution and the autonomy statutes.

The Spanish government, then, was prepared to agree to administrative decentralization but not to independence, which most Basques in any case did not really want. The Basque Nationalist Party (PNV) and the more extreme, leftist, and separatist (*abertzale*) parties together got only 35 percent of the Basque provinces' votes in the June 1977 legislative elections. One of those provinces, Navarra, was not even sure it wanted to join in the eventual Basque regional arrangement. The PSOE achieved a narrow margin over the PNV and the UCD came in third. In the March 1, 1979, elections the PNV and the *abertzale* parties together increased their vote to 44 percent of the total, but the *abertzale* were still at only 21 percent.

However, for emotional as well as political reasons, the Basque nationalist leadership wanted to leave the possibility of independence at least open, and to continue references to it as a goal. In February 1978, during one of my periodic visits to our consulate in Bilbao, I had dinner with a number of PNV leaders.* Over brandy after dinner, one of them asked if I would favor the erecting of a statue of liberty in the Basque country. I said I certainly would if it had the name of Spain on it. I agreed with the idea of decentralization; after all, the United States is a federal nation. But I did not agree with Basque independence. Another, younger leader said his father would not have liked that answer. He explained that his father had won the Silver Star in action with the United States Marines but had returned it when the United States cozied up to Franco. He quite vehemently conveyed the Basques' resentment of Franco, their lack of confidence in the current central government in Madrid, and their desire for independence. There seemed to be little question about his commitment in principle to eventual full independence. All of the others there seemed more moderate, however.

The Killings Continue. Despite the more moderate views of most Basques, there are some who clearly do want to achieve, or try to achieve, complete independence for the Basque country—and, what is more, a radical communist Basque society—as soon as possible and through whatever means necessary. These Basques, few in number, comprise the military wing of the ETA and at least a part of the *abertzale* parties of the extreme Left. They are dedicated to armed struggle—terrorism, that is—in order to achieve Basque independence. Some also want to achieve a socialist or communist state of a more uncompromising nature than anything Santiago Carrillo would immediately contemplate. These latter radical advocates of violence reject both the PNV and the PCE as too moderate and gradualist. They believe the working masses have sold out and have been sold out. The existing structure of society, they think, must be torn asunder by violence and rebuilt along their prescribed lines.

The violent wing of the ETA is acting out its beliefs through continuing and increasing terrorism. From 1968 through 1977, according to official data, the ETA was responsible for 74 killings and law enforcement officials in turn killed over 50 alleged members of the ETA. But in 1978 alone there was a total of 97 killings, of which the ETA was charged with 60.†. The rest

---

*Part of my job as deputy chief of mission was to supervise the Consulate General in Barcelona, the consulates in Seville and Bilbao, and consular agencies in Tenerife, Fuengirola, Valencia, and Mallorca. For purposes of supervision, and also better to know and test the pulse of the various regions of Spain, I visited the Consulate General and the consulates once or twice a year.

†Robert P. Clark, *The Basques, the Franco Years and Beyond* (Reno: University of Nevada Press, 1979).

were divided among the Madrid-based terrorist group, GRAPO, the political Right, and the police. In 1979, total killings rose to over 120, according to official estimates, with the ETA accounting for the larger part of them. The 1978 figures included two senior military officers, a judge, a leading newspaperman, and business and political figures as well as police. In 1979, those assassinated included a Supreme Court judge, Madrid's military governor, and an army major. In addition to killing, the ETA is exacting tribute in the form of revolutionary taxes, or protection assessments, from businesses in the Basque country, and has damaged with dynamite a nuclear plant under construction at Lemoniz, near Bilbao. Business confidence is declining, investment tends to go elsewhere, and the economy as well as public security and the general state of well-being in the Basque country are adversely affected. Business failures are numerous, while unemployment, at 14 percent, is almost double the national average. Both developments contribute to disaffection among the youth.

THE DISEASE OF TERRORISM

What is one to think when, after the death of Franco, the holding of free national legislative elections, the freeing of all political prisoners including those held for blood crimes, and the reaching of agreement on an interim autonomy statute, terrorism and general public-order problems increase markedly rather than decrease in the Basque country? Most of the political issues on the basis of which terrorism was condoned by many are now gone, but the disease of terrorism seems to wax rather than wane. Why? What to do?

The far Right and some in the military have what seem to them very clear answers to these questions. The most prominent leader of the far Right is Blas Piñar, who evokes the memory of Franco at rallies of the Right, who rants against the government, who calls for the end of permissiveness, who is referred to by some of his followers as El Caudillo (The Leader), as Franco was, and who is now a member of the Cortes, elected on March 1, 1979. He would respond to violence with violence and the return of strong central authoritarian power. He has some following; it may not be large, but it can be mobilized for demonstrations. It can also contribute toward a return to the polarization that must be avoided if the democratic experiment is to succeed. His political group is called the Fuerza Nueva (New Force), and supports publication of the right-wing newspaper *El Alcázar,* which rants against government mollycoddling and calls for law and order. Its circulation shot up in 1978, while some of the numerous milder, liberal magazines of political commentary that had been in such vogue earlier were falling on hard times. *El Alcázar* is either striking a responsive chord or else a lot of people are just curious.

There is little doubt that many Spaniards are becoming more concerned not so much about communism and the Left, although they are concerned about them despite their apparent moderation, as about public order, public morals, personal security, and national unity. The terrorism disturbs them and the Basque problem is a continual worry. But new sexual libertarianism disconcerts and discomfits them, as does the sharply higher incidence of petty crime in the cities. The military and paramilitary public-order forces in particular are uncomfortable. The military reluctantly swallowed legalization of the PCE. But many of its leaders were left with a bad taste in their mouths regarding Prime Minister Suárez and First Vice-President Gutiérrez Mellado. The military's tolerance level is being further tested by terrorism in support of not just democracy and autonomy but—it is becoming increasingly clear—in support of separatism and radical communism, coupled with an apparent general decline in public morality and order. The Civil Guard and Armed Police are directly on the firing line, and are taking casualties. At the same time they are subject to criticism for past repressiveness, and do not receive the support they feel they should have. There are symptoms of malaise that cannot be discounted. In the spring of 1978, a Civil Guard general inveighed publicly against lack of preparation and support for his forces. In November 1978 a navy captain and a Civil Guard general publicly criticized Gutiérrez Mellado and were disciplined for this act of indiscipline. In late 1978 an army lieutenant colonel and an Armed Police captain were arrested for plotting against the government. This malaise was in further evidence when, at the January 4, 1979, funeral of Madrid military governor Ortin Gil, a group of military officers seized the coffin and paraded it down the street shouting antigovernment slogans, as a crowd of some two thousand chanted, "Spain yes, democracy no."

However, the government was convinced that an unrestrained, excessive reaction against the terrorists would simply play into their hands. It was further convinced that the first objective of the terrorists was the overthrow of the existing, legitimate democratic government, and the installation of an authoritarian government of the Right that would in due course alienate the mass of Spaniards. The result, the terrorists hoped, would be a chaotic situation out of which might eventually come both independence for the Basque country and a radical government of the Left. First Vice-President for Defense Gutiérrez Mellado provided just such an analysis in a remarkable document distributed to the armed forces in November 1978. It is not Gutiérrez Mellado's style to pussyfoot, and he did not do so here. His main points were:

- The ETA's fundamental objective is destabilization of Spain's democratic regime; thus the first duty of the military is support of the democratization process.

– For the ETA, destabilization of the democratic regime is part of the process of achieving separation of and independence for the Basque provinces. This directly concerns the military. The military's principal enemy is the ETA, which is an enemy of the nation.

– The military will not achieve its objective of supporting democracy and defeating the ETA by a coup d'état. A military coup would be a victory for the ETA.

Therefore, he concluded, the discipline of the military under the King had to be reinforced.

The King himself called the military to task after the January 4, 1979, demonstration at the Madrid military governor's funeral. At a subsequent ceremony to mark the annual holiday of the Spanish armed forces, he said: "An army that lacks discipline is no longer an army. . . . The spectacle of indiscipline and disrespect caused by momentary excitement is frankly degrading."

The Government Gets Tough. The increased concern over terrorism in 1978 was reflected in a palpable change of attitude among public and politicians. In 1976 and 1977 terrorism had been condoned by many on the assumption that its presumed objectives—political liberalization and regional autonomy—were legitimate ones, and also that it was politically convenient to treat terrorists liberally because of the general public support for these objectives. All antiterrorist legislation had been swept from the books; all political prisoners had been released, including terrorists involved in blood crimes; and the police were expected to be restrained in their handling of public-order problems. But in August 1978, in the wake of increasing terrorism, new antiterrorist legislation was approved in the democratically elected legislature; and all major political parties, including the PCE and the PNV, spoke out against, and even demonstrated against, terrorism.

Armed with the new antiterrorist legislation, the government created a special counterinsurgency force and deployed it to the Basque provinces. Interior Minister Martín Villa traveled to West Germany to study that country's antiterrorist policies, and elaborated a fifteen-point program designed to suppress the ETA. In the last four months of 1978, reportedly 200 ETA members were arrested, and considerable amounts of weapons, explosives, and stolen money were confiscated. Nevertheless, some 70 ETA armed operating units, totaling perhaps 600 to 750 members, were said to be still active.*

By the end of 1978 the government was taking what would seem to have been the correct, restrained but determined, position against terrorism.

---

*Clark, op. cit.

At the same time it was trying to find acceptable solutions for any conceivable legitimate causes for terrorism by improving political and civil liberties and granting a negotiated regional autonomy. Moreover, the public and the country's political leadership emphatically and specifically rejected terrorism. The terrorists were a small group of fanatics. Ideally, in a logical world, that would seem to have been enough to solve this problem. But would it be? Unfortunately, there could be no certainty. The strength shown by the *abertzale* parties in the early 1979 legislative and municipal elections was disquieting. And it has been seen elsewhere in the world that, even with the best of will, the full employment of all legitimate means, and wide popular support, the forces of order may not be able to control terrorism completely. The British, with their long tradition of parliamentary democracy and rich experience in government, have not been able to control Irish Republican Army terrorism, to give an example. Elsewhere—Uruguay, for instance—failure of a democratic regime to control terrorism has led to loss of patience and so to authoritarianism. Thus there is the possibility that terrorism may not be controlled quickly enough by correct political, legal, and police action to forestall a reversion to authoritarianism as the antidote. This possibility raises a potential dilemma that may be described as follows.

Can Terrorism Be Controlled Without Injustice? In 1977 the Spanish government was faced with the question whether it should release from jail terrorists involved in blood crimes—murderers—for the sake of political expediency. The government wanted to be absolutely sure there could be no excuse for nonparticipation in the democratic elections that were about to take place, and no complaint that everyone was not permitted to participate in the democratic process. It therefore decided to release the terrorists. Now, looking ahead from 1979, the government may eventually be faced with another critical question. Should it go beyond the legal and moral norms of a modern democracy to control the terrorists, who are the principal threat to the new democracy and the continuing unity of Spain? The government has correctly rejected the idea put forward by some that the answer is a return to authoritarianism. But what if, after a period of time, the only real answer seems to be to lift some of the newly installed safeguards of civil liberty? Could not a legitimate argument be made that the fight with the terrorists had become war, and that during war the standards of peacetime do not all apply? The problem with this argument, where accepted, is the difficulty of drawing any logical line once the legal boundaries are passed. Antiterrorist excesses arise in response to terrorist excesses; torture and murder are committed by the public-order forces, even on the innocent; and so terrorism gains further justification for itself.

One may hope the situation in Spain does not reach a point where this crucial question will be more than academic. If all goes well, the terrorists will be controlled by legal and deflective means. Such means would include, principally, legitimate police methods, but also meeting many of the popular demands supported by both the terrorists and the Basque populace in general. They would not include concessions to the radical demands that would change the entire structure of Spanish society and the Spanish nation.

But what if the terrorists are not controlled soon through a policy of accommodation and restraint? Is a certain level of terrorist killing simply to be tolerated for an indefinite period of time? Perhaps it is, but that is not an easy or comfortable answer, just as the alternatives are not easy or comfortable. How far can the government legitimately abridge its usual legal norms in such a situation, administratively or through legislation? The dilemma is delicate, its answer is not precisely clear, and it is not unique to Spain.

SUÁREZ SEEKS AND OBTAINS A NEW MANDATE 8

The new Spanish constitution was approved in national referendum on December 6, 1978. Now that phase three of the transition had been completed, Spain and its leadership were faced with five principal political questions:

- Should Prime Minister Suárez attempt to continue to govern under the mandate of the June 15, 1977 elections for the remainder of the four-year period, until June 1981, or should he move soon to new national elections?
- If there were soon to be new national elections, what should the tactics and the focus of the preelectoral period be?
- Would the elections, when they came, produce a government that could govern effectively?
- Would these second national legislative elections, and the total process, from Franco's death on, that led up to them, produce at least two principal political parties that would be viable alternatives to govern Spain?
- What would the prospects for Spanish democracy be after this fourth phase of the transition?

THE 1979 ELECTIONS

In retrospect, Suárez' decision to hold early national legislative elections—a decision he announced promptly on December 30, 1978—was eminently reasonable. He could in theory have continued until as late as June 15, 1981, seeking sufficient margins in the Cortes by alliance with one or another splinter group as each new issue arose. But questions had arisen increasingly in the past year over the effectiveness of his leadership because of the intractability of the Basque and the terrorist problems; because of continuing economic difficulties despite the relative success of the first year of the stabilization program; because of differences over religious and educational issues and the treatment of regionalism in the constitution; and because of rising concern over issues of everyday public order and public morals. Moreover, some argued against the legitimacy of his continuing until 1981 without elections. They maintained that the chief function of the first elections in 1977 had been to produce a legislature whose principal task was the drafting of a constitution. New elections should be held to produce the legislature and the government that would flesh out and implement the constitution and govern under it, they claimed. Finally, there was a commitment to hold municipal elections soon, and, if held first, those elections could have influenced the legislative elections negatively for the UCD.

Under these circumstances, Suárez and the UCD would have had great difficulty in achieving reliable ad hoc majorities in the Cortes without confirmation of their mandate. And this difficulty was likely to have become greater, not smaller, as the success of the constitutional referendum, which gave Suárez and the government a boost for a time, receded into the past. In particular, the Suárez government might well have faced a real crisis after the municipal elections, to which the government was committed and in which the PSOE was expected to do well.

Thus the decision in favor of early legislative elections was impeccably logical. The only problem was that elections, according to the opinion polls, would be risky even in this presumably quite favorable period for the government. The polls showed the PSOE closing in on the UCD, and even perhaps passing it among those who expressed a decided view as the elections approached. The trick was that the polls also showed a large proportion of undecided voters—as much as 49 percent. Where these undecided voters would swing was the question. In this situation the tactics and the focus of the preelectoral period, with other developments in that period, could be very important in tipping the balance one way or another.

The Preelectoral Period. The stance of the UCD in the preelectoral period naturally was to defend its record. It pointed to the democratic progress that had been achieved, to the drafting of a constitution by consensus and the approval of that constitution by almost 90 percent of those who voted; to the dramatic improvement in Spain's foreign trade and international reserve position; to the decline in inflation; and to an incidence of terrorism and public-order problems that, it noted, was lower than in some other Western European countries. In all this it was treading on safe ground. The UCD's campaign was more controversial in another respect, however. The party departed from its former more conciliatory practice by saying that the time for consensus was now past; politics in Spain, it maintained, should now return to a more contentious mode. Following its own advice, it proceeded to attack the PSOE directly on its ambivalence respecting Marxism, and on its stand favoring abortion and opposing private schools.

Meanwhile, as Felipe González, at the head of the PSOE, attempted to appeal to the Center Left by projecting an image of moderation and promising "firm government" if elected, some of his associates continued to evoke the more radical, Marxist image. Moreover, both González and his Socialist companions also departed from the consensus approach and attacked the UCD more aggressively than in the past. They alleged that the UCD had failed to live up to its promises, emphasized the high rate of unemployment, and accused the UCD of "disguised Francoism." González challenged Suárez to debate but Suárez declined.

The AP, for its part, tried to recast itself in a more moderate mold by adding some personalities more inclined toward the Center than to past leadership, by sloughing off its most reactionary members, and by changing its name. When the shifting and shuffling were over, only its principal leader, Manuel Fraga Iribarne, remained from the "magnificent seven" former Franco ministers who had originally created it. Fraga was joined by Foreign Minister José María de Areilza (a fellow aspirant to the prime ministership in the King's first government), and Alfonso Osorio, minister of the presidency in the King's first government, and the three adopted the new name of Democratic Coalition (CD) for their political group. In the campaign they catered to a disillusionment with declining personal security and rising petty crime by advocating stricter law enforcement. They also opposed abortion and divorce.

The PCE opposed the idea of elections at this time because it did not believe Spain was yet ready to leave consensus politics, and presumably also because it thought it could achieve maximum influence if elections were put off. In that case, it probably reasoned, the UCD would have increasingly to look to it for support, thus enhancing its influence. It continued to call for a government of national coalition. When elections were announced and the campaign began, it naturally played up its devotion to democracy and moderation.

Two particularly noteworthy developments occurred in regional politics. Basque nationalism was clearly an even stronger and more attractive political theme in the Basque country than before, and splinter parties capitalized on it by taking more extreme positions than the PNV had on autonomy. In Andalucía, a splinter socialist group split off from the PSOE and also capitalized on the theme of regional nationalism.

While the political parties were thus positioning themselves, developments on Spain's principal problems—the economy, terrorism, and civil order—were not such as to favor the governing UCD. With all parties now devoted to politics, the government could not expect to achieve again the consensus approach to national economic problems that had been so helpful to it at the end of 1977 and through 1978. Instead it unilaterally set new macroeconomic objectives for 1979 to follow the ones that had been so well achieved the previous year. In 1978 the cost-of-living increase had been held to the target of 16.5 percent, down from 26.5 percent in 1977; a balance-of-payments surplus on current account of $1.6 billion dollars had been achieved, in contrast to a $4.3 billion deficit in the previous year; and an export-stimulated growth rate of 3.1 percent was the best since 1975. For 1979 the government set targets of 4.5 to 5 percent growth, with a further deceleration of inflation to 10 percent. In order to reduce inflation by this much, it set ceilings of 11 percent on government wage increases and of 14 percent on private-sector wage increases, against 22 percent for both in 1978. However, increases in world petroleum prices at the beginning of the year, a more militant attitude by labor (now not so restrained as in 1978 by exhortations from political mentors), and a spurt in the money supply in the first quarter, made these targets very doubtful of realization. Moreover, unemployment had risen to between 8 and 9 percent. As for terrorism, it reached a new high with elections in the offing. There were twenty-three deaths from terrorism, eighteen attributed to the ETA, in January and February alone. Among those killed, as has already been noted, were Military Governor of Madrid Constantino Ortín Gil, on January 3, and Supreme Court Judge Miguel Cruz Cuenca, on January 9. Finally, petty crime—robberies, muggings, and the like—continued to increase in urban centers; and many remembered with nostalgia the security and straight-laced moral standards of the Franco period.

Would the Elections Produce a Viable Government? In a situation where authority seemed to be deteriorating, political rhetoric was growing ever more strident, the UCD and the PSOE (according to the polls) had reached a standoff, and the PSOE itself was beset by ideological ambivalence, one could rightly wonder whether anyone would win the elections with sufficient margin and support to be able to govern effectively. Suárez and the UCD were under attack from both the Right and the Left for alleged lack of firm leadership and failure to live up to their promises, implicit or explicit. They needed to make a strong showing to regain a credible mandate. The PSOE was split ideologically over Marxism and lacked experience in public administration. Indeed, how could it have had experience? Many of its young leaders had been in jail, in exile, or in swaddling clothes while most of the UCD leaders, though also young, had been occupying responsible administrative positions, in either the public or the private sector, in the last years of Franco.

The results of the elections were a surprise in these circumstances to the pollsters and to most political analysts, and a relief, at least for the immediate future, to those concerned whether there would be a winner able to govern. The swing votes, some perhaps affected by Suárez's election-eve talk in which he attacked the PSOE for lack of ideological definition and argued that it could not be trusted, went mainly to increase the strength of the UCD and that of the nationalists in the Basque provinces and Seville. The PSOE also gained a little, but not as much as it had hoped and had been led to think quite possible by the polls. The PCE showed the virtue of moderation on the left by making some progress. The Democratic Coalition had come to moderation on the right too late and, moreover, was sadly lacking in party organization. It therefore was the principal loser in the elections. The comparative June 1977 and March 1979 election results in the Congress of Deputies are shown in table 1. In the Senate, which has less power than the Congress of Deputies, the UCD obtained an easy majority of 120 out of the 208 seats and the PSOE won 68 seats.

The elections of March 1, 1979, thus achieved for Suárez and the UCD the most that could have been hoped for: confirmation of their mandate at a level even slightly higher than in June 1977. True, they were still 8 seats short of a majority in the Congress of Deputies. But before the elections an important step had been taken to provide greater assurance of party discipline. All UCD candidates were required to submit advance letters of resignation, to be activated if they did not subsequently follow party positions in the

TABLE 1
PARTY REPRESENTATION IN SPANISH CONGRESS OF DEPUTIES, 1977 AND 1979

PARTY	SEATS IN CONGRESS OF DEPUTIES		PERCENTAGE OF VOTES CAST	
	June 1977	March 1979	June 1977	March 1979
Democratic Center (UCD)	166	168	35	35
Socialist Workers (PSOE)	118	121	29	29
Communists (PCE)	20	23	9	10
Democratic Coalition (formerly Popular Alliance)	16	9	8	5
Catalan Convergence	13	9	4	4
Basque Nationalist (PNV)	8	9	2	2
Other (including two *abertzale* parties in 1979)	10	12	13	15

legislature. Moreover, the composition of the Congress was such that the UCD could announce with confidence that it would not seek any formal coalition. Instead, it would count on ad hoc support from one or another of the smaller groups on specific issues. The Democratic Coalition (formerly the Popular Alliance), now more moderate because of the absence of six former Franco ministers and the presence of Areilza and Osorio, immediately gave Suárez a further boost by announcing it would vote for him as prime minister. Its 9 votes plus the UCD's 168 quickly gave Suárez the majority he was expected easily to have in any event.

The municipal elections followed on April 3 with results as anticipated. The UCD won by far the most councilor positions nationwide, thirty thousand as against fourteen thousand for the PSOE, and mayorships of four thousand municipalities as against fourteen hundred for the Socialists and Communists. But the Socialists together with the Communists won in most of the larger cities that account for nearly 70 percent of Spain's population, including Madrid, Barcelona, Valencia, Seville and Córdoba. While continuing to compete on national issues, the Socialists and the Communists agreed to collaborate in the elections of mayors by municipal councils. In Madrid, for instance, this collaboration gave the job of mayor to Tierno Galván, the Socialist intellectual whose small Popular Socialist Party (PSP) had merged with the PSOE earlier. One probably should not read too much from a national point of view into the victories of the Left in the major cities. Collaboration of the PSOE and the PCE at the municipal level did not, for instance, necessarily mean any change in their competitive stances at the national level. Nor would control of the municipal councils of the large cities give the Left significant additional influence on most national issues. One important exception might be public order. But on public-order issues the Left, which had a strong vested interest in the survival of democracy, might be as tough as, or tougher than, the Center. What is perhaps of greatest significance was the opportunity that the management of large cities gave the Socialists to gain badly needed administrative experience. This was a clear plus if they were to be a long-term alternative governing party to the UCD in Spain.

NEW FACES IN GOVERNMENT

After the municipal elections, Prime Minister Suárez formed a new government with some interesting changes of faces. Rodolfo Martín Villa, who had performed strongly as minister of interior, both with regard to difficult public-order issues and in organization for elections, and who had also contributed substantially to the government's overall direction, left the government entirely and was replaced by an army officer, Lieutenant General Antonio Ibáñez Freire. Martín Villa, an exceptionally able young man who had held very demanding positions for some years, doubtless could well use a rest. He would certainly be heard from again in the future at a high political level. Ibáñez Freire, as a military man who had had previous public-order experience in civil governorships—most recently in Barcelona—and as head of the Civil Guard, might do something for the morale of the public-order forces. Ibáñez also had something extra going for him: The King was said to hold him in high personal regard.

I first met Ibáñez at the house of friends in Madrid just before he received his third star, which he was not expecting. Three or four of us were congratulating another general who was known to be next in line to become a lieutenant general. I asked Ibáñez when his turn would come. He said he doubted it ever would, but then he added, "However, I will be Spain's first minister of defense." This was before the position of minister of defense existed, but when it was known that it would soon be created. Ibáñez may have been just joking. But more likely he knew he was in a position for bigger jobs by appointment. Three days later, to almost everyone's surprise, he was named head of the Civil Guard and simultaneously given the rank of lieutenant general that goes with that job. The general who was scheduled to be promoted first had to wait a while.

A civilian and former minister of industry, Augustín Rodríguez Sahagún, was named minister of defense, relieving Gutiérrez Mellado of that function; but Gutiérrez Mellado continued as first vice-president for national security and defense matters. This may have been a move to relieve Gutiérrez Mellado of some of his day-to-day administrative burdens so that he could devote more time to the important pending issue of Spain's future security arrangements. But, in addition, the bringing in of a civilian as defense minister had been envisaged for some time. The Spanish wished to follow the US pattern in this regard. Finally, Rodríguez Sahagún brought with him the special quality of an industrial background at a time when Spain had a major interest in improving its defense industries.

Francisco Fernández Ordóñez, the UCD's leading Social Democrat and as minister of finance the author of the government's major tax reform, was left out of the new cabinet. Some speculate that this was because Fernández Ordóñez was too politically ambitious, and because he was known to have had contacts on his own from time to time with the Socialists, perhaps in tentative anticipation of an alliance with them. He was another politician who no doubt would be heard from again. He won a seat in the Cortes in the elections, however, and became head of the Congress of Deputies budget committee. The man whose place he took on that committee, Jaime García Añoveros, was selected to replace him as minister of finance. García Añoveros was a highly respected economist from Seville who had also been the deputy leader of the UCD for Andalucía.

The other new appointments can be described more briefly. Landelino Lavilla, able minister of justice, moved before the full change of government to the key position of president of the Congress of Deputies, thus achieving a position marking him as a potential future prime minister. Antonio Fontán Pérez, a liberal politician who had been vice-president of the Senate, was named minister of territorial administration, a post from which he would deal with the critical issue of regionalism. He was another man in whom the King had special personal confidence. He replaced Manuel Clavero Arévalo in this function, with Clavero, the UCD leader from Seville, becoming minister of culture. Pio Cabanillas was left out of this government. José Pedro Pérez-Llorca, who had done well as the UCD's leader in the Congress of Deputies, was named minister of the presidency, and José Manuel Otero Novas, a confidant of Suárez, was given his reward for good service in the presidency by being made minister of education.

THE FUTURE OF THE UCD AND THE PSOE

The legislative elections of March 1 answered positively the principal question raised by this fourth phase of the transition. That question was whether a government that could govern effectively would be produced. But the elections did not fully answer uncertainties regarding the future of the two principal political parties. Would they be inclined to continued moderation? Would each, if elected, be capable of governing responsibly and with the support of the main political forces, and would they be reasonably assured of survival in opposition if not elected?

For the UCD, one important question regarding its future was the long-term role of Suárez himself. Would he go on forever? Had he become the indispensable man? Were there no alternatives to him as leader of the UCD should something happen to either his physical or his political health? Suárez had certainly done a remarkable job both in heading the government and in virtually creating and leading the UCD for two years. Now he had led the UCD to victory in a second and difficult national election. To some he might seem indispensable for the UCD. Certainly he would have a long career and make many further contributions to Spanish politics. But the issues still to be faced were deep, and the long-term survivability of any politician facing them was a legitimate question. Fortunately, one could see others with the potential to lead effectively should something happen to him.

To mention four, for example, reading from right to left politically within the UCD:

- Landelino Lavilla, a highly intelligent, careful, conservative workman who had had experience as undersecretary of industry in Franco's last years, had been an outstanding minister of justice under Suárez and was now in an excellent position as president of the Congress of Deputies.
- Leopoldo Calvo Sotelo, an able former businessman who is a nephew of the late conservative business leader José Calvo Sotelo, whose assassination in 1936 triggered the outbreak of the Civil War, and who has been politically active in a number of posts, most recently as chief negotiator for Spanish entrance into the Common Market.
- Rodolfo Martin Villa, an extraordinarily capable young man who had worked his way up on merit through the Franco bureaucracy, thereby gaining experience in financial and labor matters, and then was an excellent civil governor of Barcelona before serving so well as first minister of government and then minister of interior under Suárez.
- Francisco Fernández Ordóñez, a capable official in the Ministry of Finance under Franco who became undersecretary of finance and then head of the National Institute of Industries before resigning in 1974 in protest when Franco clamped down on the Spirit of February 12. Fernández Ordóñez then became the leader of a small Social Democratic group and later a capable minister of finance who concentrated on tax reform after Franco. He is a man with flair and imagination, who might be tempted to work with the PSOE under the right circumstances, but is still with the UCD.

These were four. There doubtless were and will be others.

A second basic question for the future of the UCD was whether it could stick together as a coherent party if it were to lose an election and have to live in opposition. This was a much more difficult question to answer because the UCD had originally been forged from several Liberal, Christian Democratic, Social Democratic and other groups who only reluctantly gave up their identity and accepted Suárez's leadership. They did so because that was the only way to win. It seemed likely, then, that if they were to lose under Suárez, his hold over them might slip and the party might split, in part because there were other strong personalities in it. The UCD had become a more closely knit organization with each passing month, however; and time in government thus might be on the side of its long-term survival as a single important party.

For the PSOE, the first basic question was whether it could govern were it to be elected. This question was critical to the long-term health of Spanish democracy. If the PSOE had won the March 1979 elections, the Right, including the military and the business and financial leaders, would have been very apprehensive regarding its program. Moreover, the PSOE's leadership was thin and sorely in need of administrative experience. It would have had to move very carefully and perhaps to form some sort of coalition or alliance with the UCD. After the municipal elections it fortunately won the opportunity to gain administrative experience—and a reputation for good government—from the mayoralties of the major cities. But it also—and most importantly—needed to become clearer in its ideological and programmatic purposes if it was going to both win and govern at the national level. It was highly doubtful that either the Spanish electorate or the prevailing Spanish centers of power wanted Marxist leadership then or would want it in the future. On the other hand, one could quite easily envisage the electorate wanting, and the centers of power accepting, clearly identified Social Democratic leadership at some not-too-far-distant date.

That this point was clearly understood by Felipe González was made dramatically clear shortly after the elections when, at the PSOE's national congress held in May, he resigned his secretary generalship because the congress would not support him on ending the PSOE's identification with Marxism. This did not finally decide the issue. A special congress was called for September to elect a new secretary general. Meanwhile, the PSOE was governed by a five-man caretaker commission and González continued as chief party spokesman in the Cortes.

A resounding victory for socialist moderation was accomplished in the special congress of the PSOE held from September 26 to 29. Felipe González obtained 86 percent of the votes in his contest with Marxist Luís Gómez Llorente for the secretary generalship, and swept in his entire slate of PSOE officers with him. Not one representative of the *sector crítico* (i.e., the opposition) won. With the victory of González's moderate slate came victory for his thesis that Marxism should be excised from the party's self-definition. The PSOE thus took a major step toward positioning itself as a broadly acceptable alternative for government in Spain, and toward greater appeal to the Spanish voters of the Center Left.

In so doing, both the PSOE and González were careful not entirely to alienate the party's left wing. The PSOE reaffirmed its character as a "class, mass, democratic and federal party." Yet even this left-oriented definition was blurred—one might also say contradicted—by emphasis on the need to include in the party white-collar workers, others not directly involved in producing goods, small businessmen and farmers, and professionals. The truth was that, as party leaders clearly perceived, manual laborers were now only a small part of the working class.

AFTER THE FOURTH PHASE: PROBLEMS AND PROSPECTS

The March 1979 elections produced a government that could govern and the September 1979 special congress of the PSOE produced an apparent

real, and necessary, social democratic alternative to UCD center government of Spain. Later, conceivably, another real alternative, to the right of
the UCD, might reappear. That was for the future to tell. What was important for the moment was that there were, indeed, at least two viable
political options for the government of Spain before the Spanish people.
These favorable political developments still left a number of basic issues to
be resolved. The two most immediate ones were how to deal definitively
with the pressures for regional autonomy, most importantly in the Basque
country; and how to return the economy to reasonable health.

The Statute of Guernica. In these regards, a second major positive development occurred during the last six months of 1979. It was the negotiation and approval, by referendum in the Basque region, of the Basque
autonomy statute, appropriately called the Statute of Guernica. This was
necessarily the government's first priority after the approval of the constitution in December 1978 and the elections that followed in the spring of
1979. The purpose was, first, to achieve a solution that would give the
Basques enough control over their own affairs to attract the support of the
large majority of the population of the Basque provinces; and second, to
isolate the extremists and separatists while the government maintained
enough control for the constitutional (and military) requirement of "unity of
the state." The statute worked out between the government and the Basque
Nationalist Party (PNV) provided, inter alia, for the following:

- The Basques would have a local parliament with power to pass local laws, but a
  Madrid constitutional court could nullify those laws.
- A security junta, composed equally of Basque and government representatives, would
  have police power in the Basque provinces, but the government could intervene to
  protect the "general interest."
- The Central government would not directly collect any taxes in the Basque provinces
  except customs receipts and proceeds from certain national monopolies. Instead, it
  would receive negotiated lump-sum payments from the Basque regional treasury.
  Basque provincial budgets in turn would depend largely on locally collected taxes.
- The Basques would have greater control over local schools, including the right to
  teach the Basque language, but education would remain subject to oversight by the
  central government.

This Statute of Guernica was approved within the government on
July 17, 1979, and submitted to referendum in the Basque provinces on
October 25, 1979. In the interim the ETA military wing continued to as-
sassinate policemen and government officials, and its political military wing
planted bombs in airports and railway stations. As the referendum date
approached, there was concern that abstention might be as high as 50 percent in the Basque provinces out of fear and uncertainty over the statute's
merits. However, the turnout for the referendum, despite day-long heavy

rainfall, was in fact over 60 percent of the eligible voters; the referendum was held without major incidents; and 91 percent of those voting voted for the statute in Guipuzcoa, 90 percent in Vizcaya, and 84 percent in Alava. Moreover, when a PSOE/UGT member, Germán González López, was assassinated two days later, both organizations plus the entire Communist leadership called a general strike; ten thousand people attended the funeral and later marched, with PNV and PSOE as well as other party leaders in the front lines, in protest against terrorism. It was clear that isolation of the terrorists and separatists had been achieved. It was not clear, however, that with this the terrorist acts would end.

Unfinished Business. Meanwhile no real progress was being made in addressing Spain's economic problems. Inflation continued at around 16 percent, unemployment at near 9 percent, and growth at about 2.5 percent. This was a basic issue to be carried over into 1980 and beyond. Concern also continued over terrorism and the increases in social and street crime that had accompanied Spain's democratic experiment. The list of other important matters to be addressed remained long: the decision on whether to enter NATO; the completion of military modernization; the improvement of party political organization; the development of effective regional and local elected governments; the elaboration of a new series of fundamental laws to flesh out the constitution; and the development of a consensus on such church-related matters as education, divorce, and abortion. All that would take more time, patience, will—and positive government.

There were some who wondered how much time the nation could afford. A right-wing military man, Lieutenant General Jaime Miláns de Bosch, was quoted in the November 25, 1979, issue of the *New York Times* as saying: "Objectively speaking, the balance of the transition up to now does not seem to be positive: terrorism, insecurity, inflation, economic crisis, pornography and, above all, a crisis of authority." A week previously, on November 18, a reported two hundred to four hundred thousand people had rallied in Madrid on the fourth anniversary of Franco's death.

Miláns de Bosch, though well known for his conservative views, lacked a politically strategic command position and (probably) any real support within the military. Neither his outburst, nor the nostalgia showed for the public order of Franco days by the numbers that the Right was able to rally in Madrid on that November 18, 1979, were to be taken as indications of a fatal weakening of the Spanish democratic élan. They were simply a reaffirmation, as 1979 closed, that despite the remarkable, even dramatic, progress that had been made over the four years since Franco's death, the ultimate success of Spain's democratic succession was not yet assured. The new, young leadership, like the idea of democracy, would continue to be tested until both had further, and more definitively, proven their governing capabilities.

AN ACTIVE SPANISH FOREIGN POLICY UNDER THE KING 9

In the first four years of the transition from Franco's rule, King Juan Carlos and his governments naturally concentrated on internal affairs—on the effort to achieve a stable democracy. Nevertheless, during these four years, they were also active in foreign affairs.

Spain's overall approach to foreign policy under the King is one of universality. It is Spain's desire to have at least formally correct relations with all countries. To this end, it established relations during 1976 and early 1977 with almost all countries with which it had not had relations during the Franco period, including the countries of Eastern Europe, the Soviet Union, and Mexico. One exception was Israel. To have established relations with Israel in this period would have run counter to Spain's continuing special efforts for good relations with the Arab countries. Spain's position was that it could not move to establish relations with Israel until concrete progress was made toward peace in the Middle East.

Within the overall policy of universality, Spain sought a more intimate and integral relationship with Europe, as well as strengthened relations with Latin America and the Arab World. However, despite this policy and these emphases, Spain's first priority under the King continued to be to maintain a close—though lower-key—relationship with the United States.

RELATIONS WITH EUROPE

Very shortly after Franco's death the King's first foreign minister, José María Areilza, the Count of Motrico, began a series of visits to European capitals to set the stage for closer relations between Spain and the Europe that had been so aloof during Franco's time.

Areilza, an impressive, silver-haired figure, is the ultimate in urbanity, as well as a persuasive advocate in several languages. He is also an ambitious, hard-working man, who habitually arises early in the morning to write, to read, and to prepare for the day's engagements. He is known as being a demanding superior and for keeping a full and tight schedule. Madrid's working hours had been notorious for being skewed toward the night. Senior executives tended to arrive at their offices at about 11:00 A.M., have lunch from 2:30 to 5:30 P.M., continue work until 8:00 or 9:00 P.M., and then go on to receptions beginning at 8:00 P.M. or dinner beginning at 10:00 or 10:30 P.M. But he changed that for the Foreign Ministry by himself arriving at the Foreign Ministry before 8:00 A.M. and insisting that the dinners he hosted begin promptly at 9:00 P.M. and end at 11:00 P.M. or shortly thereafter. He succeeded in changing the hours for the Foreign Ministry, but not for the rest of Madrid. True, some moving up of hours had occurred in response to a faster economic pace and greater concentration on industry and business. More executives went to their offices early. But the lunch and dinner hours had only moved up by perhaps a half-hour each. The result was a need to learn to live on very little sleep and an extraordinary desire to hibernate on weekends.

On the occasions when I met with Areilza, in my home before Franco's death, when he was still in opposition, or in his office when he was Foreign Minister, I found him a man who had clearly in mind what he wanted to say and the time he wished to allot to saying it. He was at home in the capitals of the world, having served as ambassador to Argentina, the United States, and France, and traveled extensively otherwise. Areilza's driving work habits must have disconcerted a number of his Spanish diplomatic colleagues and subordinates over the years, especially in earlier, quieter times in Spanish foreign affairs. But not all of them. There is the story of a diplomat in the Spanish Embassy in Buenos Aires who was known for his casual approach to his work and his excellence in other pursuits, including writing and the art of conversation. This diplomat asked for a month's leave to visit his ill mother in Spain. The request was granted. He arrived in Spain just before his mother's death, helped arrange for her funeral and the handling of her estate, and was ready to return well within the month. But he saw many friends and was enjoying the long conversations over coffee or brandy in the cafés of Madrid, with the result that he did not return to Argentina until two months had passed. During his prolonged absence, Areilza asked impatiently from time to time why he was not back at his desk. When he finally did return, Areilza was away for the day, but the wayward diplomat's colleagues told him he could expect a thorough dressing down from the ambassador when he arrived the next morning. The diplomat was in his office much earlier than usual the following morning, even before the ambassador. When

Areilza entered, his first sight was of his tardy staff member, whose name he immediately spoke aloud in surprise. Before he could say anything more, his man, not in the least disturbed, stopped him—and broke up the office on-lookers, but certainly not Areilza—by saying "What a good memory you have for faces, Mr. Ambassador!"

Now, on his visits around Europe as foreign minister, Areilza articulated in his inimitable manner Spain's democratic intentions under the King, and its desire for membership in the European Economic Community (EEC). His interlocutors listened with pleasure and received him with a cordiality not offered to any Spanish foreign minister for decades. They could be pardoned a certain reserve in terms of concrete commitments, however, for they were almost as aware as he that his prime minister, Arias, was not so committed to, or certain of, Spain's democratic future. This reserve continued through the early days of Prime Minister Suárez. Perhaps it may best be illustrated by a comment made to me by a British diplomat during this period. He said that, whatever the logic, the official reaction of Her Majesty's Labour Government to the democratization process in Spain would be determined, not so much by the fact that national elections were held, as by whether the Spanish Socialists viewed those elections as being free and fair in every respect. This comment pointed to a basic and still nagging un-certainty, since it was made at a time when the Socialists and the Suárez government were hotly debating electoral law modalities, and the Socialists were also insisting that the elections could not be full and fair without legalization of the Communist Party, an issue yet to be decided. However, the elections of June 15, 1977, more than satisfied the Socialists, and re-moved all political doubts on the part of the Europeans. After the elections Spain was thus free to apply for membership in the EEC without fear of rejection on political grounds. This it did in mid-July 1977.

There was and is a strong national consensus in Spain for entry into the EEC; and Spanish entry doubtless will occur in due course, with Europe being now disposed in principle to receive Spain. Nevertheless, for economic reasons, negotiations will be long and tedious. On the one hand, Spanish industry will not wish to give up protection quickly. On the other hand, European agriculture—particularly French and Italian citrus fruit and wine producers—will be reluctant to be exposed to free competition from Spain. In this regard, Spanish Communist leader Santiago Carrillo is said to have commented to President Giscard d'Estaing during the latter's 1978 visit to Madrid that while it appeared that Spain was, indeed, now no longer sep-arated from the rest of Europe by the Pyrenees, it still seemed in danger of being almost as effectively separated by the French farmers (supported, as he did not say, by the French Communists).

Another issue of special importance in Spanish relations with Europe was Gibraltar. For years Spain had campaigned for integration of Gibraltar into Spain, but Great Britain had held back, partly for military reasons but more importantly for political ones. Its official position was that it was obligated to respect the wishes of the population of Gibraltar, which was not interested in joining Spain. The United Nations asked the two countries to keep talking, which they did in a desultory fashion, but with no hope on the British side of any progress so long as the real obstacle to meaningful nego-tiations—Franco—was alive and in power. With Franco's death and free elections in Spain, the prospects picked up on this issue also. Foreign Min-isters David Owen of Great Britain and Marcelino Oreja (who replaced Areilza in the King's second government) met in Strasbourg for a first round of talks on Gibraltar, with a Gibraltarian representative present, in No-vember 1977. Subsequent rounds were held in 1978 and 1979. The atmos-phere was good and eventual compromise seemed possible.

The two European countries most interested in Spain in the post-Franco period were France and Germany. Giscard d'Estaing made a special point of attending the King's coronation ceremony, and he and the King were understood to be in touch from time to time by telephone. He was sensitive about Spain's special relationship with the United States. This sensitivity showed through in curious and at times strained protocol problems that arose over the timing and arrangements for high-level visits. From Giscard d'Estaing's point of view, there was clearly a certain amount of rivalry here. He considered Spain important and was devoting considerable personal effort to strengthening Franco-Spanish relations. He wanted France to have increased influence with Spain. Despite the reservations of French citrus and wine producers concerning Spanish entrance into the EEC, Giscard was strongly committed, at least in this period, to Spain's joining. He had been more tentative regarding the issue of refuge in the French Basque provinces for Basque militants fleeing from or exiled from Spain. There were said to be some five hundred Spanish Basque refugees in France, including a good number of extremists. In February 1979, however, the Spanish achieved a breakthrough with French authorities when the latter rounded up a score of wanted refugees and handed them over to Spanish police.

Germany's special interest in and impact on Spain were evident in the number and frequency of visits back and forth between the two coun-tries at all levels of government, and also in the frequent contact between Willy Brandt—outside the German government—and Felipe González. Brandt was thought to have considerable influence on González, and conceivably might be a factor in González's eventually leading the PSOE to its own Bad Godesburg Declaration. This would, of course, be of central importance.

RELATIONS WITH LATIN AMERICA AND THE ARAB COUNTRIES

We now turn to two other regions with which Spain has had traditional cultural and political bonds, namely, Latin America and the Arab countries. The King visited both regions. On his initial trip abroad after becoming King, he made a special point of stopping in the Dominican Republic before arriving in the United States. Subsequently, he made two more trips to Latin America. He was very warmly received wherever he went in this broad region of such great nostalgic interest to Spain. Prime Minister Suárez made his own Latin American trips, stopping in Mexico on his way to the United States in May 1977 and later going to Cuba and to Venezuela. The Spanish government has attempted to add substance to these high-level visits through increased technical assistance, cultural exchange, and credit and trade flows; but to a limited extent in most respects.

Spain's foreign policy efforts in the Arab world have encountered more difficulties. From 1975 through 1978 these efforts had three purposes beyond the traditional one of improving relations in general: more financing; avoidance of further problems with Morocco after the Madrid Accords, under which Spain disengaged from the Sahara; and neutralization of Algeria when it became a thorn in Spain's side over the Canary Islands. Spain's efforts toward these ends achieved only limited success.

The financing obtained was not exceptional. Fortunately that became somewhat of a moot point after the stabilization program, begun in the latter half of 1977, began to take hold. Soon there was a reflow of capital from abroad to Spain for normal private market reasons.

Relations with Morocco were good on the surface, but the Socialists were very critical of the Act of Madrid. Moreover, there was no certainty that Morocco would hold off indefinitely from applying pressure on Ceúta and Melilla, the two exposed Spanish enclaves in Africa that might next prove appetizing to Morocco. Spanish feeling that these two enclaves were and should continue to be an integral part of Spain ran high. King Hassan of Morocco from time to time implied that eventually he would move against one or both. After the success of his Green March on Spanish Sahara a sort of temporary truce over Ceúta and Melilla seemed to develop under which he indicated he would not press this matter as long as the Gibraltar issue was not decided for Spain. But one could not be sure, and in any event, what was Spain supposed to assume would happen regarding Ceúta and Melilla after an agreement on Gibraltar was eventually achieved?

The most difficult Arab problem of the period for Spain, after disengagement from the Sahara, turned out to be containment of Algeria's diplomatic attacks on the Canaries, two provinces of Spain off Africa's west coast. Algeria supported a movement for these islands' independence led by a Canary renegade named Antonio Cubillo. Presumably Algeria was prompted to make life difficult for Spain over the Canaries by its interests in the Maghreb, and by its view that Spain had abandoned Spanish Sahara to Morocco without due regard for the interests of either the indigenous population of the Sahara or of Algeria. Because of this view, and because of Algeria's continuing jockeying for position with Morocco, Algeria supported the POLISARIO guerrilla movement in the Sahara against both the Moroccans and the Mauritanians; also supported Cubillo, who worked out of Algeria; and promoted the cause of Canary Islands independence in the organization of African Unity (OAU). The Algerian support to this minuscule independence movement was most embarrassing to Spain and prompted it to initiate an all-out diplomatic counteroffensive in Africa. Spain's diplomatic activity, together with the inherent weakness of the case for an independent Canary Islands, seems to have carried the day. But relations between Spain and Algeria, never the best anyway in view of the different foreign and domestic orientations of their regimes, were strained by the Canaries issue to say the least.

RELATIONS WITH THE UNITED STATES

The adoption of the principle of universality in foreign relations, stronger ties with Europe, and efforts for closer relations with Latin America and the Arab countries provided a certain degree of balance to Spain's close ties with the United States. But, as I have said, relations with the United States still continued to be the centerpiece of Spain's foreign policy.

After the death of Franco, the King and Foreign Minister Areilza made conclusion of the Treaty of Friendship and Cooperation their first priority. The King's first trip abroad as king—except for his appearance before his troops in Spanish Sahara—had as its principal purpose visiting the United States, although, as we have seen, he stopped in Santo Domingo on the way. The treaty was a broad document, covering a wide range of scientific, cultural, and economic relations, as well as military matters. Contacts on all these topics were continuous in 1976, 1977, and 1978, and there were also frequent consultations and exchanges of information on international issues beyond the purely bilateral. The treaty called for twice-yearly meetings of the US secretary of state and the Spanish foreign minister and normally concurrent meetings of the US chairman of the Joint Chiefs of Staff with his Spanish counterpart. The meetings were usually held alternately in Madrid and in the United States. Since detailed matters of treaty implementation were, in the main, handled effectively at lower levels, and the general principles of the relationship between the two countries had been well established for the life of the treaty by the treaty itself, the meetings were chiefly useful as an opportunity for personal contact and discussion.

Spain had a greater operative interest than before in a wider range of foreign policy matters, and it welcomed and valued the opportunity to have periodic discussions at high levels with the United States. In one particular case, moreover, that of Algerian support for the Canary Islands independence movement in the OAU, Spanish Foreign Minister Oreja sought and readily obtained from Secretary Vance US diplomatic support for the Spanish position. Nevertheless, as I have suggested, there was the clear attempt during this time to establish a lower profile for Spain's relations with the United States as part of the better balance in Spain's total foreign policy. Neither the fact nor the appearance of overdependence on one superpower was deemed desirable. The psychologically based tensions that could develop from such dependence were evident in what Foreign Minister Areilza describes as strident and unbalanced military criticism, in cabinet-level meetings on the treaty, of the relationship with the United States. In a diary that he kept at that time Areilza says of a meeting of the chiefs of staff presided over by the King:

> Long, passionate military diatribes against the United States, read rapidly. The resistance the agreement with the United States awakens in these men is curious, considering how much they get out of it. Without United States cooperation, dating from 1953, what would have become of our armed forces? Where do their parades, maneuvers and exercises come from? The only one who dares say the truth is the minister of air: he does not want them to leave Torrejón because then there would be nowhere to put Spain's air defense wings, since Spain alone could not maintain the base. That is all. They talk of neutralism, of closing the bases, of breaking relations, of anything. I try to convince them that the agreement is part of a whole and that in today's political-military context Spain must not vacillate in cooperating with the West. Carlos Arias reminds them that Franco not only had approved the framework agreement but told the negotiators that in the last analysis they should sign whatever was put before them because Spain needed the agreement.*

Such tensions were also evident in the Socialists' well-known reservations about relations with the United States, although they, too, had additional reasons for coolness (mainly, the United States' close relations with

---

*Diario de un Ministro de la Monarquía (Barcelona: Editorial Planeta, 1977), p. 45. It is noteworthy that the Spanish air force and navy were the principal military beneficiaries of the agreements on bases. The army got considerably less out of them, had less intimate relations with Americans, and tended to be more critical.

Franco). The government well understood the desirability both of continuing close relations with the United States and, from an internal political point of view, of playing those relations in lower key and very carefully. Consequently, foreign policy speeches coming out of the government tended to be long on Europe, Latin America, the Arab countries, and the Third World, and short on references to Spain's still most fundamental relationship. Consequently also, the Spanish government took great care to interpret the Treaty of Friendship in strict terms, so that its leaders could not be open to charges from either within the government or outside it of weakness in dealing with the Americans. The government's rhetoric and posturing both represented the relationship as less important than it really was and—as is common when one nation or person becomes overly dependent on another—betrayed psychological and political resentment at its importance. This problem was not unexpected by the United States. We had anticipated that there would be this type of feeling, and that it would be accentuated after Franco's passing. We had thought the logical answer, one that would both satisfy Spain's security needs (as well as ours) and ameliorate the pains of dependency, would be Spanish membership in NATO. This was, in fact, precisely what the Spanish government wanted. Additional arguments for NATO membership were that it would give Spain a greater voice in European political, as well as military, affairs, and provide the Spanish military with the clear defense mission that they needed.

However, the Spanish government found itself faced with a peculiar situation. The PSOE, which presumably should have been even more concerned over dependence on the United States while being equally interested in Spanish national security, was opposed to Spanish entrance into NATO. The explanation of the party's position in this regard may have been, in part, that the Socialists had not yet fully and completely thought through the security issue; indeed, there was evidence of this in initial formulations on security by some Socialist leaders. In this situation, it was best for the government not to press the issue prematurely. The matter was not urgent in any event, compared with the internal matters of, first, elections and, then, constitution writing. Moreover, the treaty with the United States covered Spain's external security needs at least until 1981, when it was due for renewal, renegotiation, or expiry. The Socialists and the Communists were willing to leave the matter of Spain's ultimate security arrangements on one side while priority internal matters were being dealt with. Therefore, to the convenience of all political groups within Spain, the issue of NATO membership was not fought during this period.

THE UNITED STATES AND THE EMERGING SPANISH DEMOCRACY 10

The main interests of the United States in these initial years of the political transition in Spain were three. The first was to support the democratic evolution under the King; this had to be done without intervening or seeming in any way to play favorites among democratic parties within Spain. The second was maintenance of a constructive defense relationship under the 1976 Treaty of Friendship and Cooperation. The third was preparation of the ground for soundly based longer-term cooperation between Spain and the United States at all levels—no matter what democratic political party might be in power in Spain at any given time.

SUPPORT FOR THE DEMOCRATIC EVOLUTION

One may coldly ask why the United States should have been so interested in supporting efforts to achieve democracy in Spain if relations with the late dictator had been so clearly supportive of US security. Surely, in the new, democratic Spain, the security relationship was less clear-cut, more ambiguous, more hedged. Indeed, some within the United States government may have had that question in the back of their minds. One high US official is said to have suggested to Spanish officials at the beginning of the transition (although I have no certain knowledge he actually did) that they might try to achieve a one-party political system, à la Mexico, to avoid the potential incoherence and uncertainties of multiparty politics. Another official is said to have cautioned them to move deliberately and carefully in the process of democratization. Whether the latter suggestion, if indeed made, was poor advice or just good sense depends on what was meant. Certainly it was good sense if it meant the six months that a Spanish churchman had told me was the maximum acceptable period was too short a time. After four years, with the process not yet complete but going remarkably well in the view of most advocates of democracy, it is clear that six months provided enough time only for a beginning.

There is a twofold answer to the question of why the United States should have supported the democratic effort in Spain if relations with the dictator had been so good. First, the foreign relations of the United States do not prosper by military security alone. Our fundamental respect for and belief in democracy must be clear in what we do abroad as well as at home if we would be true to ourselves. The Carter administration has reminded us of that anew. Second, the security relationship itself will be more soundly based for the long term if founded on a democratic consensus than if derived from the will of one man—provided, of course, that there is a reasonable chance for the success of democracy.

The proviso is important in theory, but was not critical in the Spanish case. Democracy's time had come in Spain. It was going to be tried in one way or another, sooner or later, whoever was in power, so strong was the idea. And its chances were good, so fundamentally positive had been the changes in Spain over the past fifteen years. After the first weeks of the King's reign, this became increasingly apparent even to doubters across the sea; in the United States, those who had hesitated to accept the democratic effort in Spain as either valid or worthwhile were soon convinced of the opposite. Secretary of State Kissinger, who probably had been a skeptic earlier, set the tone for the future with his words at a press conference in Madrid; the occasion was the signing of the treaty with Spain in February 1976, two and one-half months after Franco's death.

> Today's event [the signing of the treaty] comes at a moment when Spain is undergoing the excitement, the inspiration and the challenge of a new era. It is my hope that this treaty will be seen as a clear sign of our moral support for Spain at this particular time. This country faces the delicate task of striking a balance between evolution and stability as it moves forward on the new course which is being charted. I have the greatest confidence that the proud and dynamic people of Spain will successfully meet the tasks that lie ahead and that Spain will increasingly enter the mainstream of those values that link the Western World in common cause....
>
> I have already explained our reason for submitting it to the Senate as a treaty, which is to reflect the increased formality and range of relationship which has been designed in the background. The reason on the American side is that in the new period that Spain is entering and in the evolution that we are encouraging, we want to reflect the sympathy and moral support of the United States.

Support for the belief that we were in fact on the right road was provided to me by the editor of a leading Spanish magazine at lunch one day. He said the image of the United States in Spain was now a good one because we seemed to be supporting Spain's political liberalization process and were also adopting a lower profile in other parts of the world. If we continued these policies and also showed ourselves to be strong advocates of civil rights around the world, he thought our future relations with Spain and with the rest of Europe would be very good for a long period of time. Strong practical demonstrations that our democratic process really worked, like the Watergate denouement or the rise of Carter without benefit of organized party support, were also helpful. In fact, he thought the tendency of Europeans to criticize the United States, basically because it seemed so large and overbearing, would soon change, and that European intellectuals would, within the next five to ten years, move more to criticism of the Soviet Union and Marxism.

These were welcome words, coming as they did from a man left of the Center. Nevertheless, the relationship with democratic Spain was a delicate one, and for the sake of sound long-term relations we had to be careful how we managed our side of it. We had to be sure we did not appear to be intervening when we merely wanted to be helpful. We had to be sure we did not appear to play favorites among the democratic parties. We had to continue the effort to improve contacts and understanding with the Socialists, in particular. Of all the democratic parties they distrusted us the most because of our past intimacy with Franco, and they were the clearest near-term alternative to the UCD as the governing party. We had also to be sure we lived strictly within the letter of the treaty with Spain; this was the only way to assure maximum cooperation and goodwill from, and minimum political embarrassment to, the Spanish government. Finally, and very importantly, it was in our interest, at the same time, to provide as much information as discreetly possible on NATO not only to the Spanish government but to political leaders outside the government. They needed such information in order to prepare for the ultimate debate on whether Spain should enter NATO.

THE NEED FOR AN AMBASSADOR FOR THE SEASON

Clearly, it was critical that our diplomatic mission in Spain be led capably and by a man attuned to the politics of this delicate period. Yet only by merest happenstance it was. That such matters are so chancy is unfortunately characteristic of our system—or, better said, lack of a system—for preparing and selecting ambassadors. Here is what happened in the Spanish case at the end of 1974.

Admiral Horacio Rivero was asked to give up his ambassadorship to Spain in November 1974. He was a far better ambassador for his time than those who decided he should leave would admit. His contacts at the top of the Spanish government were excellent. He was well acquainted with many of the Spanish leaders, including Franco, from his period as NATO naval commander for the Mediterranean. He had immediate access to Franco and anyone else in the government whom he wished to see. Franco doubtless appreciated talking to a military man, and the story goes that he also particularly liked the idea of being able to look the American ambassador directly in the eye; Rivero was as short as—perhaps even shorter than—Franco himself. In addition, having been one of our country's top military men, Admiral Rivero had no trouble commanding the respect, loyalty, and cooperation of the US military representatives in Spain. Moreover, he was an intelligent and shrewd observer, who studied Spain and its leadership carefully. He was an intellectual with command experience.

But there were two drawbacks. First, he was not given to reporting—except orally, during his periodic trips to Washington—on his knowledge of Spain and the valuable information he obtained from his contacts. He evidently did not think Washington officials needed to know as much about what was going on in Spain as they thought they did. He seemed to feel he was and should be in charge of the US mission in Spain to the same extent as he would be in charge of naval forces as a commander at sea. And he was also concerned about security if too much was committed to the written word. But the voracious bureaucracy in Washington took the lack of reporting from him as an indication that he was not on top of things.

Secondly, and more fundamentally, he was a man of the Right, identified with the now-fading Franco tradition. The importance of this factor was not so apparent at the time Rivero was removed, when Franco was still very much alive, as it was, in retrospect, when Franco died a year later. Moreover, Rivero was in fact adjusting to signs of change in Spain. He personally had some contacts with the Spanish political opposition to Franco, and he authorized members of his mission to have broader contacts than his immediate predecessors had permitted. Nevertheless, seen from the present, 1974 was a good time for a change to a new American ambassador with a more liberal image.

Fine. But that was not what Washington had in mind. The first man proposed as a replacement for Admiral Rivero was a New York banker, Peter Flanagan, who had been Nixon's top White House aide on international economic matters, and whose main connections in Spain were among the business, banking, and social elite of the Franco period. Flanagan had

had no experience with foreign political or military matters—our two main interests in Spain—and he and his banking family were firmly identified with the Franco past. If 1974 was no longer the time for Admiral Rivero as ambassador to Spain, certainly neither was it the time for Peter Flanagan.

As it turned out, Peter Flanagan did not go to Spain. But the reasons had nothing to do with foreign relations. Instead the Senate indicated its reservations because of a domestic conflict-of-interest issue that related entirely to Flanagan's past functions on the White House staff, and Flanagan himself asked that his name be withdrawn. The State Department then proposed an outstanding career Foreign Service officer, Wells Stabler, who was nominated and approved by the Senate. Stabler had made his reputation in the earlier years of his career as one of the service's best political officers in the Near East and Europe. Then he had been deputy chief of mission in Rome, and senior deputy assistant secretary of State for European Affairs. He had caught Kissinger's eye in Washington because of his adroit handling of the Cyprus crisis during and immediately after the Turkish invasion. He was an able officer with just the right political, political-military, and area experience for the job. But the fact that he was finally appointed to the Madrid embassy reflected no particular credit on the way the United States goes about selecting and appointing ambassadors. He was appointed simply because there was no strong political candidate handy at the moment, and because Kissinger happened to know him and to think highly of him.

MORE ABOUT THE UNITED STATES FOREIGN SERVICE

The United States Foreign Service performs our government's diplomatic, consular, cultural, and informational functions abroad. It is relatively small, consisting of only about 3,600 Foreign Service officers (FSOs), some 900 Foreign Service information officers (FSIOs), and associated administrative and secretarial personnel. Foreign Service officers are expected to spend about 60 percent of a normal career abroad and 40 percent in the United States. Abroad they manage some 260 US embassies, consulates general, and consulates in over 130 nations. At home they serve primarily in the State Department or the International Communications Agency.

Foreign Service officers normally concentrate during much of their careers on one of five principal kinds of work: political or political-military, economic-commercial, informational-cultural, consular, or administrative. When abroad, the political officer gathers, analyzes, and reports information on domestic political and foreign policy developments in the country in which he is serving. He conveys and interprets US policies and interests to

officials and others of the host country, makes representations, and negotiates. The political-military officer performs similarly with regard to military matters having political implications, and also has a coordinating function
concerning such matters. The economic-commercial officer does parallel
work with regard to economic and commercial matters, and provides information to and assists American exporters and investors. The information
and cultural officers concentrate broadly on providing information on the
United States and its policies to the media and to key persons of the country
in which they are stationed, and on managing cultural and educational exchange programs between the United States and that country. The consular
officer issues (or denies) visas to foreigners wishing to travel to the United
States, issues passports to Americans, and provides protection and welfare
services to Americans who encounter problems abroad. The administrative
officer provides budgetary, fiscal, personnel, communications, and general
support to the entire diplomatic mission. The two principal purposes of
these several activities of Foreign Service personnel abroad are: (1) to
anticipate, report on, and recommend policies and action concerning developments that may affect US interests in foreign countries; (2) to supervise, coordinate, conduct, and support programs, representations, and negotiations advancing US interests.

When in Washington, FSOs are assigned to offices that process and
use the information and recommendations supplied by US diplomatic missions overseas; that assist the secretary of state and the president in developing foreign policy plans and courses of action; and that provide instructions, guidance, and administrative backstopping to missions. Some
FSOs are assigned from time to time to other government agencies in the
United States, or—for training or experience—to universities, private companies, or state or local governments. The diplomatic mission abroad is
made up of much more than the relatively small number of FSOs and
support personnel assigned to a particular country. It includes all US government personnel in that country, except for those military personnel under a
specific military command. It thus may encompass, in addition to diplomatic, consular, information, and cultural personnel from the Department of
State and the International Communications Agency, any or all of the
following: army, navy and air force attachés; military assistance personnel;
economic assistance personnel; agricultural, treasury, commercial, and labor
attachés; CIA, Drug Enforcement Agency, and FBI personnel; and others.
These representatives of other US government agencies normally outnumber
the State Department Foreign Service personnel at any given post, often
greatly. All consulates or consulates general in a country are part of the one
US diplomatic mission to that country.

Overseeing the entire diplomatic mission is the ambassador. He is the personal representative of the president and as such has overall supervisory and coordinating responsibility for all US government employees in the country, except for military personnel under an operational command. Even with regard to them he is expected to provide policy guidance. His management responsibility is thus sizable. It is added to his primary tasks of informing and advising his government, and of representing his country and its interests effectively before the host country's government.

Immediately below the ambassador in the mission hierarchy is the deputy chief of mission, who is the ambassador's alter ego and acts in his stead during his absences. When the ambassador is out of the country, the deputy chief of mission becomes the chargé d'affaires ad interim, which simply means that he is temporarily, but formally and in fact, in charge of the mission. Next in line are political, political-military, economic-commercial, information, consular, and administrative counselors, various attachés, and other agency representatives—all under the overall supervision of the ambassador.

The size and composition of diplomatic missions varies with the extent and variety of our relations with each country. Our mission in Spain is fairly large, reflecting the significance and reach of our relations with that country. It ranged between four and five hundred in complement during the time I was there, about half Americans and most of the remainder Spanish support employees. Given the significance of military matters in our relations with Spain, it is not surprising that a considerable part of this total consisted of military personnel.

Clearly the specific areas in which a diplomatic mission concentrates will vary according to the United States role in the world at that point in history, the situation in the particular country where the mission is, and the state of relations between that country and the United States. For instance, in Latin America during the period of the Alliance for Progress, economic development was the major focus of our diplomatic missions there. In Southeast Asia during the 1960s, our missions necessarily concentrated on issues connected with the Vietnam War. Currently our principal focus in Japan is on its economic policy. In Spain from 1974 to 1978 the main interests of our mission, as I have said, were the democratic transition and the security relationship between our two countries.

While the principal issues concerning an individual diplomatic mission may be clear, they are obviously not the only matters to be dealt with. Sometimes events occur that overnight preempt the mission's time and energies, changing its overall focus for a while. Such an event, for instance, was the nationalization of the International Petroleum Company (IPC) in Peru in October 1968, when our mission there had to shift its primary concentration from economic development to investment protection. The IPC problem had been vying with economic development for the mission's attention for some time in fact, but after October 1968 the mission perforce had to focus principally on it and on other similar investment issues that developed.*

In Spain, an event that changed our mission's principal focus briefly but drastically was the crash of two jet planes—Pan American and KLM—in Tenerife on a Sunday in March 1977, when 320 Americans were killed. I was chargé at the time, and enjoying a rare quiet evening at home. I had just told my wife that having finished all the odd jobs saved up for the weekend, I was bored. Then, at 8:00 P.M., the telephone rang. It was our public affairs counselor relaying the first reports of the tragedy. From that time until I went to bed at about 1:00 A.M., to get a little rest, the numerous phones in our residence rang continually and a considerable portion of the mission staff, as well as all my household, was mobilized to meet this emergency. Tenerife, in the Canary Islands, was far away and hard to get to; communications were not good and the reports were confusing. It obviously was important that US embassy personnel arrive on the scene of the accident as soon as possible to help survivors, provide accurate information to all concerned, and coordinate actions leading to the identification and proper disposition of the victims' bodies. There was no immediate means of getting from Madrid to Tenerife by commercial airline. I therefore arranged for the US military group chief's small plane to take a task force of essential personnel to deal with the problems that would be faced. Since the accident had occurred on the runway and caused the Tenerife airport to be closed, the plane would have to go to Las Palmas (on a neighboring island) and a helicopter or ferry would be used to transport the task force from there to Tenerife. I asked the administrative counselor, a cool and experienced officer, to lead the task force, which included two consular officers, the air attaché, a doctor, the press attaché, and a secretary. By midnight this task force was on its way to Las Palmas, a flight of some five hours. Meanwhile, I arranged for a Madrid-based task force to be on twenty-four-hour duty to maintain communications with the United States and elsewhere on the matter, and to deal in the first instance with the multitude of questions and issues that would inevitably arise. The State Department organized its own emergency group to provide backstopping for us and to communicate with all those concerned in the United States.

When I finally went to bed at 1:00 A.M., I was reasonably confident that I had done all that was possible for the time being. But at 5:30 A.M. I

---

*If for no other reason, because of the Hickenlooper amendment to the 1961 Foreign Assistance Act, which required that foreign aid to any country be cut off if there were not reasonable steps toward prompt, effective, and adequate compensation for expropriated American properties.

was awakened by the embassy duty officer to be told there was no trace of the plane that had left Madrid with our task force. I asked myself what I had done. Had I sent nine more people off to die? But that type of thinking was futile; I had done what had to be done. An hour later the news came that the embassy's plane was safe on the ground at Las Palmas, and that the task force was on its way by ferry to Tenerife.

For the next forty-eight hours most of the diplomatic mission in Spain was committed to dealing with this tragedy. No one was spending much time on Spain's political transition or on our military relations with Spain; an emergency consular protection-and-welfare job had taken first priority. All available assistance was provided to the survivors: teams came to identify the dead; accident investigators arrived to work with Spanish authorities; families and the public were kept informed and appropriate coordination with Spanish and Dutch officials was maintained. By Wednesday, military planes brought in from our European command had departed Las Palmas for the United States with the dead and some survivors. By the end of the week most members of the US mission were back at their usual functions, although some had follow-up consular and investigative work to do for weeks thereafter. The State Department gave the task force members who worked on this case superior honor awards for what it termed an exemplary response to an emergency. Bureaucracies sometimes are self-serving and too easily self-congratulatory in matters like this. I took particular satisfaction, therefore, in comments made to me two years later by a pastor from the community in which perhaps fifty of the Pan American passengers had resided. He said that all concerned families with whom he had discussed the tragic crash had been unanimous in their commendatory remarks about how our diplomatic mission in Spain and the State Department in Washington had handled the matter.

The Trouble with (Some) Ambassadors. The US Foreign Service is a small group of talented, hard-working, dedicated men and women who perform well day in, day out, in emergency or routine, over an exceptional range of functions. Nevertheless, the service has problems, and there is considerable room for improvement. One set of problems concerns the selection and advancement of its personnel. The selection process at the beginning level is not a cause for concern. The written and oral examinations are rigorous, and the service is able to accept only 1 to 2 percent of those who take the examinations each year. It should therefore be safe to assume that virtually all entering officers have good potential.* There is, however, a

---

*Nevertheless, there are usually gaps in background that need to be filled. Periodic refreshers, then, should be provided through improved training programs after entry into the service.

considerable shadow over personnel selection at the top of the service. It is the continuing practice of filling between 25 and 30 percent of ambassadorships with political appointees, some of whom are clearly not as competent as trained senior FSOs. I would agree that there is justification for naming some highly qualified ambassadors from outside the service. They can be particularly effective if their special expertise is intimately related to the country to which they are assigned, and also if they are personally close to the president and have his confidence. But the number of potential candidates for ambassadorships from outside the service who are really outstanding and who are available is likely to be small at any given time. Moreover, the morale of the many career officers who aspire to be ambassadors, and who believe themselves to be as well or better qualified than the usual political appointee, suffers seriously when they see duds appointed from the outside to positions they know they can handle better, and for which they have spent a lifetime of preparation. All things considered, perhaps 10 percent would be a reasonable proportion of ambassadorships to be allocated to political appointees rather than the current 25 to 30 percent.

Some past political appointees have been classic Ugly Americans. There was, for example, the appointee of a Democratic administration who wrote top-secret telegrams based on quotes from an English-language newspaper from a neighboring country because he did not know the language of his host country. Another was the appointee of a Republican administration whose greatest contribution was a series of ideas for improving the advertisements of one US firm in the country where he was assigned. Another who couldn't speak the language of the country he was accredited to was convinced, seriously it seems, that his special mission as ambassador was to change it to English. There may be fewer of this type now. But despite President Carter's early declarations of intent to the contrary, the quality of his political appointees to the service has not been universally high, and the number is too large.

The problems of selection at the top of the Foreign Service do not end with the undue number of political appointees and the questionable quality of some of them. There also should be improvement in the selection of ambassadors from within the service. This problem has two principal facets. One is a matter of undue expectations. The other is the question of what are the most important criteria for ambassadorial appointees.

There was a tendency in the past to give every entering FSO the idea that he might become an ambassador. This was clearly a delusion, not only because so few ambassadorial positions were available, but because some functions in the career do not prepare an officer to be an ambassador. The idea in the mind of all FSOs that they should become ambassadors naturally resulted in undue pressure on management to name ambassadors from all functional categories of the service. It also resulted in a sense of frustration for many FSOs, despite the fact that Foreign Service life and work, in whatever specific function, are interesting, varied, challenging, and usually stimulating. The answer to this problem is simply a greater element of frankness. I am glad to note that beginning officers are now told that most of them will not advance beyond the class three level, which is equivalent to colonel in military rank. As it becomes better understood within the service that achieving this level is a considerable accomplishment in itself, and would be viewed as such by most outside observers, the morale of the service in this regard should improve.

If few Foreign Service officers can expect to become ambassadors even though they enter the service under highly competitive circumstances, what special qualities should those who reach the top possess? I would emphasize four, in order of importance: (1) ability to develop relations of confidence with the official and private leaders of the country to which they have been assigned; (2) analytical and judgmental capability in the political, political-military, and economic spheres; (3) balance and integrity under pressure; (4) management talent. (That they should also have knowledge and understanding of their own country goes without saying.) The first quality is the most necessary one. This is not sufficiently recognized by those who decide on ambassadorships. They tend to rank bureaucratic (or political) considerations too high, forgetting that the principal job of an ambassador is to deal effectively on substantive matters with the leaders of the country to which he is assigned. In developing relations of confidence at the top, no one can really substitute for the ambassador except for the highest officials from Washington, and they do not have the time to perform this ambassadorial function in many places or over prolonged periods. Ideally, of course, the ambassador should be strong in all four respects.

THE ISSUE OF US POLITICAL IMPARTIALITY

To return to US-Spanish relations during the transition, the issue of presumed US favoritism toward one political group, with all that this implied, came to a head in a *Washington Post* story of July 1976. The text of the pertinent part of the story follows.

U.S. OFFERS TO SUPPORT SPAIN BAN
By Miguel Acoca
Madrid, July 29

U.S. Secretary of State Henry A. Kissinger has told Spain's King Juan Carlos that the United States would back his government if it chose to go slow on extending the benefits of democracy to the still-outlawed Communist Party according to informed Spanish sources.

Kissinger reportedly told the King that it is up to Spain to decide to legalize the Communist Party but that Washington would not object if this were to be put off until after the first free parliamentary elections since the Spanish Civil War of the 1930s.

The royal government has pledged elections before mid-1977.

Kissinger, according to the sources, told the King that he recognizes that Spain is under pressure from French, British and Dutch officials to speed up the democratization process if Spain is to gain its long-sought membership in the European Common Market and the Atlantic Alliance.

But, Kissinger reportedly said, the United States would help to prop up the badly lagging Spanish economy to make up at least temporarily for Spain's lack of freer access to West European markets. The Common Market already buys about 40 percent of Spain's exports.

Kissinger's message was interpreted by his Spanish listeners as meaning that Washington would like the King to bend his efforts to insure the control of Parliament by moderates.

The Secretary spoke to the young King at least twice at some length during the monarch's Bicentennial visit to Washington. One of the conversations was completely private.

The sources, some of whom had direct knowledge of the talks, said that the King listened to Kissinger's view of how to deal with the Communist problem in Spain with attention and respect, but that he later expressed concern that the Secretary might not be the one directing American foreign policy by the time the Spanish elections take place.

The Secretary reportedly told the King that moderate political control of the first post-Franco Parliament is vital not only for stability in Western Europe but in Africa and the Mediterranean because of Spain's strategic position, the sources said.

Secretary Kissinger reportedly told Juan Carlos it was not necessary for Spain to rush into a break with the Franco institutions to join the Atlantic Alliance, the sources said. . . .

The story was prompted in part by a widespread impression in Madrid that Secretary Kissinger had urged and was urging the Spanish leadership to go slow on democracy, and in part by the belief among some that Ambassador Stabler, with his background in Italy, was actively favoring the Christian Democrats. Both speculations were so wide off the mark that the State Department spokesman volunteered the following denial and correction.

We do not usually discuss the contents of official, private conversations with leaders of other governments, but the story from Madrid in this morning's *Washington Post* contains a highly inaccurate account of the Secretary's conversations with the Spanish King and of U.S. attitudes and policy toward Spain.

We have always taken the position that it is up to the Spanish government to decide the pace and the exact nature of changes in Spanish institutions.

It is not true that the Spanish King was told that it was not necessary for the Spanish to rush into a break with the Franco institutions (whatever that means).

We have publicly and privately taken the position for some time that we favor a strengthening of moderate political institutions in Spain and moves which the Spanish government has announced toward the creation of democratic institutions.

The question of legalizing the Communist Party is an internal matter for the Spanish government to decide and that is the position we have always taken. However, in our judgment it would be absurd to make legalization of a party dedicated to authoritarian principles a litmus test as to whether or not democratization is taking place.

I can also flatly deny that the United States government supports or has been helping to finance the formation of a center right party. The United States is not supporting any particular party in Spain and our statements have been limited to general support for a strengthening of the moderate political spectrum. United States economic relations with Spain are a matter of public record as is our willingness to help Spain with its economy.

No new commitments were made during the King's visit and there was no suggestion for the United States taking measures to make up at least temporarily for Spain's lack of freer access to Western European markets.

With regard to our position concerning the democratic political parties, the fact was that the Madrid embassy was continuing its efforts to maintain and expand contacts with the leadership of all such parties, without favoring any particular one. With reference to the Communists, we did deliberately maintain a distinction. Our contacts with the Communists were only at the level of a junior or middle-grade officer in the political section and with Communists who were not members of the party's central committee. We had contacts with democratic parties at all levels. This distinction symbolized our higher regard for democratic parties.

MAINTENANCE OF A CONSTRUCTIVE DEFENSE RELATIONSHIP

Strict adherence to the letter of the Treaty of Friendship and Cooperation was, as we saw in chapter 9, a matter of some political importance to Spain. But it was hard for our military forces in Europe to understand. They thought it obvious that the clear mutual security interests of our two countries would call for flexibility in military access to and use of Spanish bases. They remembered that the pattern of the past under Franco had been for Spain readily to grant considerable flexibility. Issues frequently arose over the use of base facilities, issues that would seem small and easy to resolve in terms of pure security interests, but were delicate in the political context for Spanish authorities. The limitation of the number of tankers at Zaragoza air base to five at any one time was one case in point. Another was the definition of "standby basis" for the Morón air base, and the need to exercise the base from time to time to make sure it could be of use when needed. Still another was how often nuclear-powered warships should visit Spanish ports and under what circumstances. Such issues required constant monitoring by policy officials in the embassy and continuous close contacts with Spanish officials. The United States mission accordingly set up its own clear lines of authority and coordination on treaty matters; there was constant committee work under the treaty structure, as well as supplementary informal contact with the Spanish. It was hard, detailed, sometimes onerous work, and not everybody's wishes could be met. But the job was done in such a way, I believe, that the Spanish received a sense of frankness, openness, and commitment to cooperation on our part, and they responded with the level of flexibility they honestly believed could be justified.

The relationship was made the more difficult by the fact that the Spanish military, the army in particular, had never been convinced that the United States was as forthcoming in the provision of materiel—in amounts, quality, or level of sophistication—as the military relationship and our mutual interests under the treaty called for. This issue arose repeatedly, and was complicated by the fact that although the United States had a treaty relationship with Spain it did not automatically give Spain the same consideration on provision of arms as it did the NATO countries and some other allies. Therefore each case of provision of arms over which there was any question had to be fought out individually within the bureaucracy, with inevitable delays, uncertainties, and tensions. NATO membership would have been a neat way to resolve this problem, but Spain was not yet ready to decide on that. As it was, our military relationship with Spain was helped by a visit to the United States, in the summer of 1978, by Vice-President for Defense Affairs Gutiérrez Mellado, who took part in frank discussions on arms transfer and other issues of military cooperation. The bureaucracies on both sides responded a bit better after that, although problems still remained.

The main problem with regard to NATO membership, as we saw in the previous chapter, was the Socialists. They seemed to be seeking a situation of independence from both superpowers through a strictly European defense force of some sort. When it was explained to them, through their contacts both with Europeans and with us, that the United States would itself have liked a European defense force and at one time had tried for one, but that it had proved impractical because of intra-European problems, they were somewhat at a loss as to where to go from there. Negatively, they referred to their concern that Yugoslavia would feel under greater pressure from the Soviet Union if Spain joined NATO, that Spanish membership in NATO would be a provocation to the Soviet Union, that NATO didn't pay enough attention to the Mediterranean and to North Africa, and that NATO membership would cost too much. These reservations on NATO were reinforced by senior military concern, particularly in the army, that NATO membership would be too much of a challenge for Spain in terms of military competence and also costs. None of these arguments answered the fundamental question of how Spain was to bear its part of the Western defense burden if indeed there was a threat to the West from the East as was assumed. Nor did they demonstrate how Spain could reach its political potential within Europe if it did not specifically join Europe militarily, as well as economically. Moreover, they rejected the thesis of deterrence. They seemed to postulate that the Soviet Union would respond to weakness with weakness, a risky idea. In general, they gave the impression of wanting above all to deny that a threat existed.

The Communists seemed somewhat ambivalent. They were against military pacts in principle, but wanted to maintain independence from the Soviet Union. They did not want to destabilize the military equilibrium, and accepted US troops at Spanish bases so long as troops remained in Eastern Europe. They referred to NATO as providing a shield against Soviet interventions. But they were skeptical about NATO in some regards, and Santiago Carrillo talked about the desirability of a regional European defense arrangement.*

It was not yet a time for decision. It was, instead, a time for discussion, for exchange of information and maturing of views on NATO. Under the treaty structure there was an "ad hoc committee on NATO," of which I was a cochairman, which served as a major conduit for information on how

---

*In *Eurocomunismo y Estado,* after alluding to the military hegemony of the two superpowers, Carrillo expresses doubt about the credibility of the nuclear umbrella and says (p. 93): "From this well-founded doubt arises the idea of a European defense force, and may arise new concepts of regional defense that may be inevitable on the road to a new world order based on general disarmament. . . ." Spanish policy in military matters must be flexible, he continues (pp. 138–39); it should not destabilize the present equilibrium of forces or risk Spain's passing from American to Soviet influence. But a European defense arrangement, independent of both the United States and the Soviet Union, might be convenient even for the United States. After all, given its nuclear power, the United States does not need the Spanish bases, he says.

NATO operated, what its assumptions were, and what the advantages and costs to Spain might be. We could not, of course, speak for NATO or other NATO members. Therefore we had to be careful to make it clear that we were providing illustrative, hypothetical information. Additional informal exchanges went on with technicians and political leaders—all looking forward to the time when Spain would ultimately make its decision. Meanwhile the United States made it abundantly clear that, although it favored Spanish entrance into NATO, it was not pressing Spain. The US position, stated simply and repeatedly, was that the decision on whether or not to join NATO was Spain's to make, at the time it chose to make it.

It was difficult for many Spanish to believe that the United States would take such a relaxed position on Spanish entrance into NATO. This was illustrated during a brief visit to Madrid in the spring of 1978 by Senate Majority Leader Robert Byrd. The senator was on a trip to other countries of Europe, at the request of the President, to stress the importance we gave to NATO. In Madrid, his purpose was quite different: he simply wanted to underline the importance we gave to Spain and to the success of its democratic transition. We advised him to stay away from the NATO issue in Madrid because of its political delicacy, and he followed that advice to the letter. He did not once mention NATO in his conversations with Spanish officials, including Prime Minister Suárez. At a number of points during the conversation the prime minister clearly left openings for the discussion of NATO, but the senator did not take advantage of them. Finally, I whispered to him that the prime minister obviously wanted to talk about NATO. The senator whispered back that he knew that, but he was not going to mention NATO because he wanted to be able to say to the press later that the subject had not come up. As he left the prime minister's residence, the reporters gathered outside repeatedly asked him about the talks they presumed he had had with the prime minister about NATO. And he repeatedly left them speechless and floundering for other questions by saying the subject had not arisen. Later a Spanish official asked me quizzically if I didn't think we were overdoing our position a little.

United States–Spanish relations throughout 1976, 1977, 1978, and 1979, the first four years after Franco's death, on the whole were excellent. They were certainly better than one might have expected in view of the shadow of our past close relationship with Franco. This was due primarily to strong basic mutual interests and to the moderate orientation of the Spanish society of the 1970s. The Spaniards of the immediate post-Franco period were not interested in radical departures in either domestic or foreign affairs.

But that was not the whole story. On the Spanish side our good relations also resulted from the positive view of the United States held by the

King and by other top government leaders, including Prime Minister Suárez and Foreign Ministers Areilza and Oreja; and, I would submit, from competent management of the United States official business with Spain. Special recognition should go, in this regard, to the professional leadership of Ambassador Wells Stabler as chief of mission for much of that period, and to the similar professionalism of Ambassador Terence Todman, who followed him.

THE FORCES OF FREEDOM IN SPAIN: THREE SCENARIOS FOR THE FUTURE 11

Franco maintained control in Spain and served his country as he saw best until his last day on earth, as he had vowed he would. He was, almost to that day, still the principal political arbiter in Spain, as he had been for forty years. But in his latter years, and particularly in his last months, another political force quite antithetical to his beliefs, the idea of democracy, gained rapidly on him. It was there ready to replace him at the moment of his death, as the controller of Spanish political events for the immediate future. When he did die, the idea was translated into the political and social modalities and institutions needed for its implementation through the efforts of a remarkable new, young generation of leaders headed by, but not limited to, King Juan Carlos and, after an interval, Prime Minister Adolfo Suárez.

FORCES STRENGTHENING THE DEMOCRATIC IDEA

But what gave such strength to the idea of democracy and such vitality and innovative drive to the new, young leadership? It was, first, the economic and social progress of the fifteen years before Franco's death. This progress transformed the Spanish society, including the attitudes and capabilities of its people. The middle class grew greatly in size and in political and social importance. The more industrialized, more urbanized, more pluralistic society that accompanied the economic and social advance required—and gained—different skills, different types of preparation, greater mobility, greater adaptability. The focus was now much less on the individual's traditional place in society and more on the individual himself, on how he responded to a more fluid and more diverse ambiance. Responsibility rested more on each separate human being than on any previously established hierarchy. Ironically, Franco abetted the process by his own belief in meritocracy. He had himself advanced rapidly in the military on the basis of merit. He believed this was the way institutions should work. Therefore he insisted that in his Spain the first in the class should get the best job. He also abetted it in the latter part of his rule by his support of progressive social programs—broad social security coverage, more funds for education, a degree of agrarian reform, and higher wages.

Old institutions and old patterns perforce changed. The family, the community, the church, the military, and the traditional social and political elites had less authority. The church, responding perhaps more to Pope John XXIII than to what was happening in Spain, itself liberalized. The educational system expanded and had to become more technical, empirical, and scientific. Both basic literacy and the quality and variety of educational opportunities increased enormously.

The destabilizing earlier stage of economic development, when the main psychological effect can be an unsettling greater awareness of differences in status, passed to a new stage in Spain, a stage in which much of the populace could be reasonably satisfied with the material and social results of development. The youth of all classes had new economic, educational, and status opportunities beyond anything most of them or their parents might have dreamed of in earlier decades. The average Spaniard now had a stake in the future. Spain was no longer just two Spains, the privileged and the poor; there was now a third Spain, a Spain of the middle class and of opportunities—and it controlled.

The average Spaniard now had a new confidence that led him not only to question past ways and authorities more assertively, but also to raise his sights: with basic survival assured, he aimed first at simple material needs and then at greater political liberties. And some Spaniards, given new opportunities and stimulated by new challenges, proved not to be average at all but rather the stuff of modernizing, liberalizing leadership. Taking nothing away from the dramatic and remarkable performance of Juan Carlos and Adolfo Suárez after Franco's death, had they not been there others would, I believe, have led Spain on essentially the same route, although probably without such sureness of foot. The system and the circumstances were producing the type of innovator required to implement an idea whose time had come.

The second reason why democracy prevailed was that there were in Spain no traumatic cleavages or crises—such as severe racial or cultural inequalities or the shock of defeat in a colonial war that so affected Portugal—that were perceived to demand extremist solutions implemented through authoritarian means. Regionalism and terrorism were known to be difficult problems, but they did not seem, at least at that time, to be of sufficient magnitude to defy democratic solution or, if solution was too much to expect, to doom the democratic experiment.

Thirdly, the successful example from abroad of the politically liberal, mixed-economy systems of the world's advanced industrialized countries—an example rubbed in by the persistent standoffishness of the Western European democracies in the face of Spain's continued authoritarian regime—added its special contribution. And the unsuccessful example, both politically and economically, of the still totalitarian and austere communist countries did likewise. Santiago Carrillo, though a Communist, made this latter point most tellingly in *Eurocomunismo y Estado* in his discussion of the extraordinary economic and social progress in the industrialized democracies as contrasted with the backwardness and repression in the Soviet Union.

And then the idea of democracy was strengthened, fourthly, by the passage of enough time. There was time for the changes in the society to occur and have their effects. There was time, also, for the passions of the Civil War and its immediate aftermath to cool, and for concern over the chaos and polarization after the last experiment in democracy to recede a bit, but not enough time to eliminate the moderating effect of that concern or to produce a new polarization and extended violence born of political frustration.

THE SUPPORTIVE ROLE OF INSTITUTIONS

But the idea of democracy and the new liberalizing leadership could not have functioned and prospered alone, in a vacuum, without the needed institutions—essential organizations and accepted procedures—to support and implement their purpose. Such institutions were needed for channeling the ever more diverse forces of a rapidly modernizing society into coherent compromise and effective government. They could be old institutions adapted to new ends or new institutions created for new objectives. Some—the monarchy, the church, (surprisingly) the Franco Cortes, the judiciary, some political parties, some incipient labor organizations, the media—not only existed already at the point of transition, but also performed positively and contributed in various ways to a sense of legitimacy. Some—the military, the police forces and the civilian bureaucracy—were established institutions with long traditions and well-established procedures that carried out their assigned functions, but were not enthusiastically responsive. Still others—the constitution, the center and left political parties, the electoral law, democratically elected local governments, and some interest groups—had to be established and are as yet to be fully tested.

The Monarchy. The monarchy was the lead institution. It was invaluable in legitimizing the succession, providing direction and impetus, and setting the tone for democracy. This might not have been the case. All indications were that Franco had trained Juan Carlos with the idea that he would preside over a continuation of Francoist authoritarianism rather than a democratic transition. Juan Carlos had given little prior indication of the strength of his democratic orientation or of his leadership capabilities. Moreover, the monarchy did not have solid popular backing. But the young king surprised everyone with his commitment to government at the will of the people and his strength of leadership. By exhibiting these characteristics, and by trips around the country that permitted the people to know him and his family better, he broadened his popular base. And, at the same time, he worked hard to retain a close relationship with the military, which historically had played a strong political role up to the time of Franco, and might again.

What of the monarchy's future? The King fully recognized that in a constitutional, parliamentary democracy he should, over time, be less directly involved in government; he should continue to set the tone, he should reign, but he should not rule. His intimate involvement in major personnel and government decisions was essential during the first years of transition. It should be less so in the future, however, as the modus operandi for parliamentary democracy becomes better established. But the temptation for the King to assert himself will be strong, and decisions on where to draw the line will not be easy.

The Prime Ministership. Franco's delegation of the prime ministership in the last years of his life was helpful. It established the custom of day-to-day government leadership below the level of chief of state. Initially, after Franco's death, the prime ministership was a problem because of Arias's indecisiveness. Had Carrero Blanco lived, it would have been a greater problem for the opposite reason—overassertiveness. But once the holdover premier was removed, and a pragmatic political innovator responsive to the King installed, it became a distinct plus.

The Military and the Police Force. Historically the military has been the final arbiter of the political process in Spain. Under Franco, who ruled more like a king than a military leader, it was largely apolitical, however, except in its support of the regime and of national unity. Franco saw to that by keeping it divided, by not permitting any single military leader to become a potential competitor with him for political power, and by governing principally through civilian ministers. It has since accepted the transition to democracy and the leadership of the King as the legitimate chief of state and commander-in-chief of the armed forces. Its acceptance is uneasy, however. It is uncomfortable with the legalization of the Spanish Communist Party (PCE), with the degree of autonomy sought by some regions, particularly the Basques, with rising public-order problems both from terrorists and from petty criminals, and with the relaxation of public morality. The military desires reassurance and needs modernization—as well, perhaps, as a new sense of mission. The military is in process of reorganization, but has not been reassured; reorganization, in fact, can be more unsettling than reassuring in its early stages. And the military's future mission has not yet been fully determined. It will not be determined at least until Spain reaches its decision on whether or not to enter NATO.

The police forces are at a low point in morale because of both political and terrorist attacks on them. Clearly steps are needed to improve the situation. The reinstituted antiterrorist legislation of 1978 and the more determined antiterrorist actions of late 1978 and of 1979 should give some boost to police morale. But the terrorist problem is proving deep, grave, and persistent.

The Bureaucracy and the Legislature. The civilian bureaucracy is traditionally well organized in a series of services (*cuerpos*), each with its own entry and promotion discipline. It could help greatly in day-to-day government, but not so greatly in innovative new approaches.

The King and his first government avoided a confrontation with nostalgic Francoists by using a number of institutions of the past, most notably the holdover Cortes, to legitimize both the modalities and the holding of the first free legislative elections. The new, freely elected legislature provided the political leaders who drafted and then approved the constitution. The new parliament has not as yet been a significant source of legislation otherwise. Instead, it has been a forum for debate, expression of the views of political groups, and endorsement of government initiatives. To be effective, it will need to take more legislative initiative itself in the future.

The Political Parties, Local Government, and the Constitution. Among political parties, those that lived underground for decades—the PCE and the PSOE—are best organized, although both have had identity problems forced on them by a contemporary Spanish society that rejects radical revolutionary answers. Both the PSOE and the PCE have thus far been strong vehicles of protest against the political straitjacket of the past, as well as responsible supporters of the democratic process. Their moderation and their responsibility show that they understand the conservatism of a majority that is largely satisfied with the social and economic system as it now functions. Equally clear is their belief that the best opportunity for them to influence modern Spain is through democracy. They have not wanted to provoke confrontation and polarization, to attempt revolution, or to risk return to jail, exile, or clandestineness. For democracy to be consolidated and continue over the long term, they must maintain their moderation in the face of temptations to return to the more extreme and more confrontational patterns of the past.

The governing center party, the UCD, has made some organizational progress, but needs to make more. It depends too much on the charisma and leadership of one man and on being in government. This is easily explainable in view of the political habits of the past forty years. It is natural at the beginning. It can change only with time.

It is probably true that the durability of Spanish democracy will not receive final confirmation until the UCD has been tested in opposition and the PSOE has been tested in government. Parliamentary democracies need a credible potential for responsible periodic alternation of political leadership between at least two major political groupings. Otherwise, the group too long in power loses its will and ability to innovate, and the public becomes frustrated at the lack of opportunity for change or renovation. The first opportunity for alternation in government by Spain's two principal political parties—the March 1979 legislative elections—passed with no change. Perhaps this was just as well, because it was not clear either that the traditionalist forces were ready for a socialist government or that the Socialists were yet well prepared or even eager to govern. But the Socialists will have the opportunity to gain considerable experience over the next few years, both as the major opposition party and through their leadership of Spain's main cities, where they gained the balance of power in the April 3 municipal elections.

Democratic local political structures are being tried for the first time and have therefore yet to prove themselves. Symbolic establishment of regional governments has occurred, but not yet significant devolution of powers. The newly elected governments of the municipalities have just come to office.

The d'Hondt electoral law has been a positive factor in forcing a reduction of the number of political parties and thus making more likely the election of governments that can govern effectively. The law has its critics, but it was agreed upon through negotiation among the political groups and is not under strong attack.

The constitution is now in place. It has the virtue of being not an academic scroll imposed from above, but a consensus document that is the product of compromise among the principal political groups. It does not completely satisfy anyone, and it offends some traditionalists. Nevertheless, the hope is that it is sufficiently responsive to the majority and sufficiently flexible to last longer than Spain's many other past constitutions (for which see appendix C).

The Labor Organizations. Labor is in a period of definition. Under Franco, an attempt was made to establish a corporate structure in which labor, management, and government would work harmoniously. Over time, however, parallel labor organizations developed, mostly in secret. Some were supported by the Communists or the Socialists; some by the Catholic church; some had an anarchist heritage; and others were independent and apolitical.

After Franco died, the government under Juan Carlos decided to encourage labor pluralism and independence rather than attempt to maintain a corporate structure that was, in any event, no longer sustainable. Thus far the communist-oriented Workers Commissions have had the lead in labor organization, followed closely by the socialist-oriented General Workers Union. There are still many unions independent of these two organizations, however, and, in fact, many workers who do not belong to any union. The UCD is encouraging independent unions sympathetic to but not affiliated with it. Labor has, on the whole, supported the democratic process, even to the extent of accepting wage restraint in 1978 under a stabilization program the success of which it saw as important to the success of democracy. In the early 1979 preelection period, however, since the previous political consensus on stabilization targets had not been reaffirmed, it became more assertive of its particular interests, with the result that there was a rash of strikes. It has thus shown itself to be democratically oriented, at least in the short run, but with a measure of self-discipline in support of democracy that is of uncertain durability. Moreover, the ultimate ideological direction of both unions and union leadership is a basic issue for the future.

Business, the Church, and the Judiciary. Business responded to the new political situation by organizing its own nationwide interest groups. In May 1976 two national business associations were formed, one to represent large enterprises, and the other small and medium-sized ones. In May 1977 a third national association was formed with leanings to the Franco past. After the June 1977 elections, the three associations merged with still another older group and established the Spanish Confederation of Business Organizations (CEOE), in order to present a united front in dialogue with the government on economic policy and present business views effectively to the public. More than one hundred business organizations representing several hundred thousand individual firms and accounting for one-fourth of Spain's industrial production belong to the CEOE. Government-owned and controlled companies are not included, and some small and medium-sized business organizations have joined a second national association, the General Confederation of Small and Medium Business of Spain (COPYME).

The Spanish church, which earlier was a conservative bastion of the Franco regime, became more liberal in Franco's last years, as did the Catholic church worldwide. It involved itself in political, labor, and social issues in favor of greater equality, greater opportunity for political participation, and even greater regional autonomy. Its leader, Cardinal Tarancón, spoke out in favor of liberalization at the time the King came to power, and the church approved of the reforms that followed even though it did not play a specific role in their elaboration. Its weight has declined in a less traditionalist Spanish society, but to the extent that it continues to have influence, it supports both social and political progress.

A judiciary with considerable reputation for independence was in place from the past when Franco died and readily facilitated—some would say too readily—the amnesties and the moves to ensure the full political participation of the left, including the communists, that followed.

The Media. Political commentary magazines and groups proliferated after Franco died; they provided a further means of interest and opinion articulation, and reveled in their new freedom. Most of them strongly supported the liberalization process that was occurring. There were some exceptions, most notably the right-wing paper *Alcázar,* which was a voice for those dubious about the performance and benefits of democracy.

Strengths and Weaknesses. Thus most of the institutions needed to make a stable democracy function either existed before the death of Franco—and, at this writing, had been adapted to new political circumstances or purposes— or had been formed, or were in process of formation. Their creation or positive adaptation followed from the strength of Spain's desire for democracy, and from the quality of the leadership that guided them in new directions or developed them where they did not previously exist. Another type of leadership, under the influence of a different idea, could have guided most of them in a quite different direction.

There are still weaknesses in political institution formation. Political party organization in the center and on the right is still only incipient. Ideological definition of the political parties of the left is still uncertain. The role of parliament remains limited; staff organizations to serve it have not yet been created. Effective representative government at the regional, provincial, and local levels has not yet stood the test of time. The mission of the military and public-order forces has not been established and their morale is low. It will require time, patience, and continued good leadership, with a continued positive attitude, to remedy these weaknesses. The monarchy, most of the political leadership, the church, most of the media, and the intelligentsia continue to be disposed to provide that leadership and that attitude. Elements of the military, business, conservative traditionalists, political extremists, and labor are inclined to question, each for its own reasons.

THE FIRST FOUR YEARS: A SUMMARY

King Juan Carlos, Prime Minister Suárez, and their governments, using a policy of openness, dialogue, compromise, and consensus beyond that customary even in most democracies and certainly unexpected in Spain, achieved, in the four years between Franco's death and the end of 1979, two national legislative elections accepted as free and fair by all, a textbook program of economic stabilization supported by all major political parties and social groups, and a constitution endorsed by 90 percent of those who voted (although the level of abstentions was ominous). They also made headway on regional autonomy arrangements, establishment of rational rules of the game for labor union organization and activity, modernization of the military structure, and diversification of Spanish foreign policy.

Much has been accomplished, but there is much more to be done. The three critical matters to be dealt with in the next phase are:

- The consolidation of the Basque regional arrangement, and the containment of terrorism.
- The implementation of responsible future economic policy, both to meet internal Spanish needs as fully as can be expected, and also to prepare Spain for entry into the European Economic Community (EEC).
- The consolidation of the moderate stances of the principal parties of the Left, particularly the PSOE, which has a special responsibility as the only currently credible alternative to the UCD for government of Spain.

Other important matters to be dealt with are a decision on whether Spain should enter NATO, correction of the institutional weakness mentioned above, and the curbing of social excesses that have arisen in the new atmosphere of freedom.

Although the forces of freedom have proven themselves unexpectedly strong in Spain in the first three and one-half years after Franco's death, warning signals have appeared that significant counterforces exist. The most dangerous of these are the regional and extreme left terrorists and the extreme right coupists. Radically different in end political goals, these two forces are united in their opposition to the system as it is now, and their activities are complementary. In fact, the strategy of the extreme Left is to provoke, through terrorism, a situation in which the Right may return to power temporarily, on the premise that the eventual reaction to the reinstitution of right authoritarianism will be a radical swing to the left. They seek to polarize the Spanish society anew, believing that in the end the left pole will be the stronger.

The terrorists of the Left and the coupists of the Right are both small in number, and unrepresentative of the sentiments of most of Spanish society at the end of 1979. They cannot succeed so long as that society and its leaders maintain confidence in themselves and in what they are doing. But the extremes of the Left and the Right are betting that eventually they will not maintain that confidence. The strongest cards held by these extremists are not their own numbers or the vitality of their ideas, but rather the potential for eventual disillusionment on the part of the rest of the population. Disillusionment can indeed come, most obviously, from the persistence of a terrorism now made more difficult, in a way, to deal with by the compunctions of a liberal, democratic society; from continuing poor economic performance after a fifteen-year boom; and from excessive relaxation of social discipline in response to greater political freedom.

Samuel Huntington has postulated that a sudden "burst of explosive energy," when civil freedoms are restored after a long period of repression, typically leads to widespread disillusionment and a conservative reaction.* Observers of Spanish history have also noted a cyclical process regarding democracy. The first cycle began with the death of Ferdinand VII in 1833. He was replaced by a liberal monarch and restricted suffrage until 1868. Then there was a democratic monarchy and universal suffrage until 1873, followed by the First Republic in 1873–74 and civil war. The second cycle began with the restoration of the monarchy in 1875. Limited suffrage was established from 1877 to 1880 and universal suffrage from 1890 to 1931. Then the monarchy again collapsed, and the Second Republic was established—again followed, in 1936, by civil war.

Huntington's postulate, and also the current Spanish situation, recall the importance of political expectations. The consolidation of democracy evidently requires a coincidence of sufficient success in dealing with a society's economic, social, institutional, and security challenges with realism in expectations. If, for instance, economic and social expectations are low, as they traditionally have been in India, progress on the economic and social fronts can be modest provided that the institutional framework is firm and security issues are in hand. If, however, expectations are high, a higher level of performance is needed.

Will Spain's future be as Huntington's postulate would indicate? Will there be a third cycle in the history of Spanish democracy similar to the first

---

Political Order in Changing Societies (New Haven, Conn.: Yale University Press, 1968), p. 407.

two? If Huntington's postulate applies, how far will the pendulum swing back to the right? And then how far the other way?

SCENARIOS FOR THE FUTURE

In this context, one may envision three broad alternative scenarios for the next ten to twenty years.

(1) *The pendulum swings back to authoritarianism.* The Basque regional problem is not resolved, despite some promising progress in the second half of 1979. Terrorism escalates, with more high-ranking figures kidnapped or killed. Capital continues to flee the Basque region. The Basque economy is depressed, while unemployment and social disaffection increase. Labor becomes increasingly restless with the economic stabilization program, which is accompanied by persistent and high unemployment. So do the political parties and leaders. The stabilization measures are relaxed and inflation accelerates. Attempts to stimulate the economy through easier credit and government spending fail. Investor confidence is lacking. Production declines. Unemployment increases further. Labor agitation increases, while the PSOE and PCE rhetoric becomes increasingly radical. Petty crime increases. The students, heretofore quiescent, begin to agitate. There is increasing concern among conservatives, not only over general disorder and lack of solution to the terrorist and economic problems, but also over laxity in moral codes and moves to make divorce and abortion permissible. The moral peccadilloes of a high government leader are exposed. Another is accused of fraud.

Democracy is seen more and more as a cause of problems rather than a means of dealing with them. Ideological extremes have stronger followings. Felipe González's victory for social democracy in the special congress of the PSOE in September 1979 is short-lived. Nostalgia for Franco-type solutions grows. The idea of a return to authoritarianism to restore order, morality, and material progress becomes increasingly acceptable—until, one day, it happens. An assertive military leader, supported by the tacit acceptance of the people, organizes a coup, deposes the King, and assumes power for an indefinite period. He has some success in restoring order, but is not able to solve the Basque problem or completely to control terrorism. He also has some success in reducing inflation and restoring investor confidence, but at the cost of alienating and eventually radicalizing labor and the intelligentsia. All the new political leadership that flourished for a time either gives up politics or goes underground. The PSOE and PCE both revert to radical ideological postures. González and Carrillo withdraw in favor of more uncompromising leadership.

In foreign affairs the new military leader is prepared to enter NATO, and from a security point of view the NATO countries would like to have

Spain in. But their political sensibilities do not permit them to respond to his willingness to join. This rejection by foreigners gives him a boost in internal popularity, but only for a time. He is too conservative even for his own caste. After two or three years of mixed success in his policies at the cost of alienation of labor, intellectuals, and politicians, he is ousted by another general with reformist leanings, supported by key middle-grade officers. This officer announces that Spain's primary internal objective will be achievement of industrial democracy through worker self-management, and that Spain's principal foreign policy objective will be independence and neutrality. Spain has no interest in joining NATO and will accept no foreign troops on its soil. His new cabinet is a mixture of the military and civilian. An aged but still spry Santiago Carrillo is minister of education. But both the PCE and the PSOE by now seem to be to the left of him; and the Peruvianization (i.e., conversion to left reformism) of the Spanish military satisfies neither at this juncture. Once again, Spain has been effectively polarized.

(2) *Spain muddles through.* Successive civilian governments deal with Spain's problems with partial success. Spain's future continues uncertain, and Spain is not a dynamic force in foreign affairs.

The Basques do not fully accept the autonomy arrangements proposed by the government, and terrorist activity continues, although at a reduced level from the 1979 peak. The Basque country is not so dynamic economically as it had been in the past, but some of its capital and its entrepreneurial skills move to other parts of Spain, where they have positive impact. Political and labor pressures lead to attenuation of the stabilization program. Inflation is reduced to between 10 and 15 percent per year, but no further. Spain eventually negotiates entrance into the European Economic Community, but its economy is chronically weak and requires continuing exceptions. Spain continues divided over the NATO issue and does not enter. It continues to have a defense agreement with the United States, but at a reduced level. The United States retains the use of facilities at Rota and Zaragoza, but Torrejón can be used only on standby basis. The Ministry of Defense becomes fully operative but other efforts to modernize the armed forces languish.

Life in Spain is not uncomfortable compared to that in many industrialized countries, but it lacks élan. The political leaders who previously attacked the country's problems with such verve and imagination seem to have lost their confidence and drive. Suárez continues as prime minister over a long period. He works hard and deals with each problem skillfully, but solutions do not come at will. The people want a change, not because he has not done well, but simply because it is politically normal for them to want periodic changes. At the same time, however, they are afraid of the alternatives, and therefore continue to reelect the UCD headed by him. There is talk of replacing him as prime minister by Lavilla, Martin Villa, Fernández Ordoñez, or Calvo Sotelo in order to give the people a sense of a new look. But this is not done. The PSOE and PCE oust González and Carrillo and become increasingly more contentious and less willing to compromise on issues fundamental to effective government of the country. There is a sense of unfulfilled expectations, on the one hand, and of malaise over the permissiveness and public-order problems of the society, on the other. But no one perceives, or implements, better alternatives; expectations have declined; and the extremes of both the Left and the Right wait for stronger pretexts to move against democracy than in fact exist.

(3) *Spain realizes a vision.* The moderate Basque leadership is given sufficient responsibility for Basque province affairs, including certain police functions, to satisfy it, and proceeds to exercise that responsibility effectively. It does not press the cause of separatism, although some still speak of separatism as an ultimate objective. Lacking popular support, in fact facing popular rejection, terrorism gradually dies down. Investor confidence in the Basque country returns, and the Basque economy resumes a measure of its previous dynamism.

The government continues firm on its stabilization path, and the level of inflation is gradually reduced to the 4 to 6 percent range. Spain enters the European Economic Community and proves to be competitive. Spain also joins NATO, and proceeds with the modernization of the Spanish military structure and armed forces.

The Spanish Socialist Workers Party continues with Felipe González as its leader. It speaks less and less of Marxism, and decides to eliminate the term "workers" from its name as too restrictive; henceforth it will aim to appeal more clearly to a broader spectrum of the society. The Socialist Party in due course achieves a plurality in elections and becomes the governing party for a time. It focuses during its incumbency on three things: maintaining Spain's economic dynamism and competitiveness; strengthening Spain's role in Europe and in world affairs; and gradually developing comanagement and cooperative programs within Spain. It does not raise the issue of Spanish membership in NATO; and in line with previous statements, it returns some nationalized companies to the private sector. Some of its leaders still speak of worker self-management as a long-term goal, and note the success of some experiments of this nature. But they also state that conditions constantly change, and that the precise pattern of future arrangements for workers to assume management functions cannot be fully predicted now, particularly in view of the evolution in importance of white-collar and service groups in modern industrial and postindustrial societies.

The politics of dialogue, compromise, and consensus rather than confrontation continue on vital issues, while there is clear competition on lesser issues; and the public becomes accustomed to alternation in power of the two principal political parties. At the same time, Spain becomes increasingly accepted as a strong, positive force within Europe.

Juan Carlos celebrates his twentieth anniversary as King by asking Adolfo Suárez, Felipe González, four other political leaders who have been particularly prominent in the two decades of constitutional, monarchical democracy, and their wives, to dine with him and the Queen to reflect on the vision they had had of what a young and dynamic Spain could accomplish, and on how that vision has matured.

THE HOPE FOR SPANISH DEMOCRACY

What will Spain's real scenario of the future be? No one can be sure. Certainly it will not be exactly any one of those sketched above. I personally believe it will be a positive scenario that will fall between numbers two and three. My belief is based on the judgments

- That the Spanish society has been so fundamentally changed by economic and social progress that it is, and will remain, in the political center, with the basically minor oscillations of the pendulum to left or right that are to be expected periodically in modern, industrialized western societies;
- That the new generation of leaders will continue to show imagination, depth, and flexibility in coping with the issues it faces, and that the admittedly difficult regional, internal-security, economic, social, and political problems the Spanish democratic government and people face will thus be dealt with in as responsible a manner as can reasonably be expected, while none of these problems will be perceived by the Spanish people as being so critical as to drive them to political extremes;
- That foreign examples will continue favorable to, and the pull of Western Europe will work positively on, Spanish economic and political performance;
- That Spanish political institutions—in particular the parties and local government— will gain strength with time and experience.
- That the Center and the Left will therefore retain and consolidate their commitment to moderation and democracy, that their combined commitment will be stronger than the negativism of doubters on the right or the destabilizing efforts of agitators at the extremes, and that democracy's imperfections will be broadly understood to be less serious than those of either leftist totalitarianism or rightist authoritarianism.

For these reasons, the idea of democracy, while less universally and unequivocally hailed now and in the future than at the beginning after Franco's death, will nevertheless continue to prevail in Spain.

CHRONOLOGY OF MAIN EVENTS

1973

December 20: Prime Minister Luís Carrero Blanco, handpicked by Franco to carry on the Francoist tradition, is assassinated by Basque terrorists. He is replaced by Carlos Arias Navarro.

1974

February 12: New Prime Minister Arias Navarro makes a major policy speech setting forth plans for mild political liberalization. They would include authorization of "political associations" (not political parties), provision for popular election of mayors and other muncipal officials, and prohibition of certain senior government officials from being members of the legislature while holding their high-level government positions.

July 19: First negotiating session, in Madrid, on renewal of the agreement on Spanish base facilities.

October 29: Franco casts a pall over the Spirit of February 12 by firing liberal Minister of Culture and Information Pio Cabanillas. Some other high officials resign in protest.

December: At Arias's insistence, the law providing for political associations is passed.

1975

May 31: President Ford visits Spain.

September 27: Five terrorists convicted by military courts of material

Most of this chronology was graciously provided by Ray Caldwell, of the US Embassy in Madrid.

involvement in the killing of police are executed. The executions are widely disapproved in Europe as evidence of continued repressiveness in Spain.

November 14: The Madrid Accords, formalizing Spain's departure from the Sahara, are signed.

November 20: Franco dies.

November 22: King Juan Carlos I accedes to the throne.

December 13: The King installs his first cabinet, with Carlos Arias continuing as prime minister, and Foreign Minister Areilza, Minister of Government Fraga, and Minister of Justice Garrigues as three major liberalizing members.

1976

January 13: Official Spanish presence in Western Sahara is terminated under provisions of an accord with Morocco and Mauritania signed in Madrid in mid-November 1975.

January 24: New Treaty of Friendship and Cooperation is signed between the United States and Spain.

February 26: Last Spanish military units are withdrawn from the Sahara.

June 1–5: The King visits the United States.

July 3: The King, having dismissed Arias, names Adolfo Suárez as his second prime minister.

July 28–30: PCE central committee meets openly in Rome.

September 22: Because of his resistance to the reform program, General de Santiago, first vice-president of the government, resigns to be replaced by General Gutiérrez Mellado.

November 18: Franco-era Cortes signs its own obituary by approving the political reform bill which, inter alia, provides for free election of a bicameral parliament with constituent powers.

December 5–8: Still-illegal PSOE holds open party congress in Madrid, with presence of Brandt, Mitterrand, Palme, Nenni, and other Socialist leaders.

December 10: PCE Secretary General Santiago Carrillo holds "clandestine" press conference in Madrid.

December 11: GRAPO kidnaps Council State President Oriol.

December 15: The Spanish people, in referendum, overwhelmingly approve the political reform law.

December 22: Carrillo and seven other PCE leaders are arrested in Madrid and charged with "illegal association."

December 30: Carrillo and the other seven are released on bail.

1977

January 24: General Emilio Villaescusa, president of the Supreme Military Justice Council, is kidnapped by GRAPO.

January 24: Ultrarightists murder four PCE lawyers and an office attendant at their Calle Atocha office in Madrid.

January 28: GRAPO assassinates two armed policemen.

February 8: Council of Ministers approves decree-law abolishing old party registration process (the *ventanilla*), and replacing it with a purely administrative-judicial proceeding. This act opens way for legalization of all major parties.

February 9: Spain and the USSR reestablish diplomatic relations. (Relations with other Eastern European countries either precede or follow.)

February 10: Decree-law abolishing *ventanilla* goes into effect. The PSOE and a host of other parties apply for legalization.

February 11: Police rescue kidnap victims Oriol and Villaescusa unharmed.

February 17: PSOE and six other parties formally legalized.

February 22: PCE legalization application referred by Interior Ministry to the Supreme Court for a decision.

March 2–3: Eurocommunist "summit" in Madrid, with participation of Berlinguer, Marchais, and Carrillo.

March 11: Council of Ministers approves measures broadening application of July 1976 amnesty and establishing a basis for individual pardons for those not covered.

March 16: Council of Ministers approves election law to govern parliamentary elections.

March 28: Spain and Mexico reestablish diplomatic relations.

March 31: Confusion ensues when Supreme Court refuses to rule on PCE legalization, returning the case to the government.

April 9: The government, in a surprise move, legalizes the PCE on Easter Sunday night.

April 12: High Army Council expresses displeasure over PCE legalization.

April 13: Navy Minister Pita da Veiga resigns in protest over PCE legalization.

April 15: Council of Ministers officially convokes elections for June 15. Twenty-one-day campaign to begin May 24.

April 22: Council of Ministers approves implementing legislation for legalization of trade unions; registration to be initiated April 28.

April 25: Suárez initiates travel to Mexico and the United States.

May 3: Suárez announces that he will run for parliament as a UCD "independent."

May 13: PCE President Dolores Ibarruri ("La Pasionaria") returns from Soviet exile.

May 14: Don Juan de Borbón renounces his dynastic claim to the throne in favor of his son, Juan Carlos.

May 23: Cortes President Torcuato Fernández-Miranda resigns, clearing the way for appointment of a new president after the June 15 elections.

May 24: Election campaign begins.

Early June: Most ETA "political" prisoners are released, the most controversial of them being sent into exile, in order to clear the way for elections.

June 15: National elections held. UCD and PSOE are the big winners.

June 17: Suárez is confirmed in his post by the King.

July 4: Suárez names his new government.

Mid-July: Spain applies for EEC membership.

August: Suárez begins series of visits to European capitals.

September 11: Over one million Cataláns demonstrate peacefully for autonomy in Barcelona.

September 29: Council of Ministers approves decree-laws reestablishing Catalán Generalitat.

October 14: Both houses of parliament approve a political amnesty law based on consensus.

October 27: PCE Secretary General Carrillo presented by Fraga at Siglo XXI.

October 25: Economic and political installments of Monclóa Pact signed.

Early November: Carrillo travels to Moscow for sixtieth anniversary celebrations; is not permitted to deliver address.

Mid-November: Carrillo and González travel to the United States.

November 20: Ultrarightists sponsor huge rally in Madrid's Plaza de Oriente to commemorate second anniversary of Franco's death.

November 24: Foreign Minister Oreja and British Foreign Secretary Owen meet in Strasburg for first round of talks on Gibraltar with Gibraltarian representatives present.

November 25: Leaked copy of draft constitution published in Madrid press.

December 6: Council of Ministers approves transitional plant elections decree.

Mid-December: PSOE delegation, led by González, visits Soviet Union.

December 30: Council of Ministers approves preautonomy statute for Basque provinces.

1978

January–April: Labor plant elections held. The Communist-dominated Workers' Commissions come in first, with about 37 percent, while the Socialist UGT runs a strong second, with about 31 percent. The independent Socialist USO is a distant third.

January 25: Former Barcelona Mayor Joaquín Viola Sauret and his wife are assassinated by left-wing terrorists.

February: GOS protests Algeria-initiated OAU declarations on "Africanness" and "colonial" status of Canaries and support for Canaries proindependence terrorists emanating from OAU summit in Tripoli. Relations with Algeria deteriorate, and the two countries' ambassadors are eventually withdrawn (the Algerian one unofficially).

February 24: Suárez shuffles his cabinet, naming four new ministers: Rodríguez Sahagún (industry and energy), Sánchez Terán (transport and communications), Lamó de Espinosa (agriculture), and Calvo Ortega (labor).

March 7: Military court in Barcelona finds El Joglars mime troupe members guilty of "insulting" the military in one of their plays; sentences defendants to two years in prison.

March 15: Second round of Oreja-Owen (plus Gibraltarian reps') talks on Gibraltar.

March 17: The Basque terrorist ETA sets off large explosive device at nuclear plant construction site near Bilbao; two workmen killed, hundreds of thousands of dollars in damage.

March 22: Director General for Prisons Jesus Haddad assassinated, apparently by the ultraleft terrorist group GRAPO.

April 10: Congress of Deputies subcommittee charged with drafting a new constitution formally concludes its task. Consideration of draft now passes to full committee, beginning in early May.

April 19–23: Spanish Communist Party holds first legal party congress in Spain since the Second Republic. PCE Secretary General Santiago Carrillo is reelected and his general policy line is ratified.

April 30: Spanish Socialists (PSOE and PSP) formalize unity.

October 19–21: UCD holds constituent congress.

October 31: Constitution ratified by Congress and Senate.

December 6: Constitution ratified in national referendum.

December 30: Parliament dissolved; national elections convoked for March 1, 1979.

1979

January 17–20: Foreign Minister Oreja makes official visit to Soviet Union.

March 1: UCD wins plurality in Spain's second legislative elections under the King, followed by PSOE, PCE, and CD/AP; on the basis of these results, Suárez forms another UCD government.

April 3: UCD wins plurality in municipal elections, but PSOE/PCE "municipal pact" places almost all of the major mayoralities in the hands of the Left (mostly the PSOE).

May 17–20: PSOE's twenty-eighth party congress concludes without election of new secretary general, when Felipe González refuses to run for reelection because of differences over "Marxism"; *comisión gestora* formed, and extraordinary congress set for September.

May 21–25: Romanian President Ceauşescu makes official visit to Spain.

September 13–15: PLO leader Yasser Arafat makes official visit to Spain and is received by Suárez.

September 28–29: PSOE extraordinary congress gives Felipe González overwhelming mandate, removes "Marxist" from party's self-definition.

October 25: Basque and Catalán voters ratify in referendum, respective autonomy statutes approved previously in the Congress.

November 19–20: Soviet foreign minister Gromyko makes official visit to Spain.

PRINCIPAL
PERSONALITIES B

ABRIL MARTORELL, FERNANDO; long-time confidant of Suárez; named minister of agriculture in the King's second government; in the third government, became vice-president for economic affairs and Suárez's most intimate and trusted collaborator.

ALVAREZ DE MIRANDA, FERNANDO; moderate Christian Democratic leader; named president of the lower house of the legislature after the first elections of June 15, 1977.

APOSTÚA, LUÍS; respected political columnist for the Madrid newspaper, *YA*; member of Congress after the June 15, 1977 elections.

AREILZA, JOSÉ MARÍA DE; urbane businessman, government official, and diplomat; King Juan Carlos I's first foreign minister.

ARIAS NAVARRO, CARLOS; former director general of security, respected mayor of Madrid, and minister of government; became Franco's second and last prime minister after the death of Carrero Blanco; began the political opening characterized as the Spirit of February 12; continued for six months as the King's first prime minister; did not adjust to the King's desires for a faster and more decided change sufficiently to satisfy the King.

ARIAS SALGADO, RAFAEL; young, able Social Democrat who became, in 1977, the first secretary general of the Union of the Democratic Center (UCD).

ARALUCE, JUAN MARÍA DE; president of the Guipuzcoa Municipal Assembly; assassinated on October 4, 1976.

BARRERA IRIMO, ANTONIO; first vice-president and minister of finance in the Spirit of February 12 Arias government; resigned in sympathy with Cabanillas.

BORBÓN, JUAN CARLOS DE; the Prince chosen by Franco to be King upon his death; has proven, presumably quite contrary to Franco's expectations, a remarkable leader of Spain in its transition to democracy.

BORBÓN, JUAN DE; Juan Carlos's father, second son and designated heir of King Alfonso XIII.

BORBÓN, PRINCESS SOFÍA DE; the King's attractive, gracious, and intelligent wife; sister of ex-King Constantine of Greece.

CABANILLAS GALLAS, PIO; Liberal minister of information and culture in the Arias Spirit of February 12 government; sacked by Franco in October 1974 for going too far too fast in freeing the press; later returned as a minister for the King, after being one of the leaders of a center political grouping.

CAMACHO, MARCELINO; Spain's principal labor leader of the Left; revealed himself as a member of the central committee of the Spanish Communist Party when that committee met openly in Rome on July 28, 1976.

CAMUÑAS, IGNACIO; leader of a small Liberal group; minister of the Cortes in the King's third government who was removed from that position because of his confrontational approach to relations with the PSOE.

CANTARERO, MANUEL; a political leader of the moderate Left who developed one of the principal "political associations" in the last months of Franco's life, but fell into the political background after Franco's death.

CALVO SOTELO, LEOPOLDO; minister of public works in the King's second government; later chief Spanish negotiator for Spain's entry into the European Economic Community (EEC); helped organize Suárez's Union of the Democratic Center in the last weeks and days before the June 15, 1977 elections.

CARRERO BLANCO, ADMIRAL LUÍS; long-time Franco confidant, and Franco's first prime minister, appointed as such in June 1973; assassinated by terrorists in December 1973, an act that hastened somewhat the pace of political change.

CARRILLO, SANTIAGO; secretary general of the Spanish Communist Party since 1960 and a leading Eurocommunist who took a position supportive of the King in the first years of the democratic evolution.

CORTINA MAURI, PEDRO; Spanish foreign minister until Franco's death in November 1975.

CLAVERO ARÉVALO, MANUEL; UCD leader from Sevilla who was minister of territorial administration after the June 1977 elections and minister of culture after the March 1979 elections.

DÍEZ ALEGRÍA, GENERAL MANUEL; chief of the Spanish High General Staff until mid-1974.

EATON, MERCEDES H.; wife of the author; native of La Paz, Bolivia; the Eatons were married in 1949, during the author's first Foreign Service assignment, and Mrs. Eaton has accompanied him on all his assignments.

EATON, SAMUEL D.; author of this book; Foreign Service officer, class I; minister counselor and deputy chief of mission at the United States Embassy in Spain from July 1974 to August 1978; deputy assistant secretary of state for inter-American affairs at the time of final editing of the book.

FERNÁNDEZ MIRANDA, TORCUATO; able product of the Franco regime who was acting prime minister briefly after Carrero Blanco was assassinated and whom the King had elected as the president of the Cortes after Franco died; one of the King's tutors when the King was a youth.

FERNÁNDEZ ORDÓNEZ, FRANCISCO; head of the National Institute for Industry and former undersecretary of finance who also resigned in sympathy with Cabanillas; led a small Social Democratic party after Franco's death; returned to be minister of finance in the King's third cabinet after the elections of June 15, 1977; as minister of finance, he pushed through a tax reform that gave the King's government credibility with the Center Left.

FONTÁN PÉREZ, ANTONIO; a liberal politician who was vice-president of the Senate after the June 1977 elections and then minister of territorial administration after the March 1979 elections.

FRAGA IRIBARNE, MANUEL; dynamic former minister of information and culture and ambassador to England; minister of government in the King's first cabinet and an aspirant to the prime ministership; later formed and led the rightist Popular Alliance (AP) in a losing cause in the June 1977 elections, and continued to be a strong representative of the Right in the Cortes.

FRANCO BAHAMONDE, GENERALÍSIMO FRANCISCO; leader of the uprising against the Spanish Republic in 1936 and then leader of Spain until his death on November 20, 1975.

FUENTES QUINTANA, ENRIQUE; highly respected economist who was vice-president for economic affairs in the King's third government and the author of the successful economic stabilization program instituted in the second half of 1977.

GALVÁN, TIERNO; veteran, respected Marxist theoretician and academician who was leader of a Socialist splinter group that eventually merged with the PSOE; later became mayor of Madrid.

GARCÍA AÑOVEROS, JAIME; economist and UCD political leader from Sevilla; became minister of finance after the March 1979 elections.

DÍAZ-CAÑABETE, ANTONIO GARRIGUES; distinguished elder lawyer, Catholic layman, and former ambassador to the Vatican and to the United States who was the King's first minister of justice.

GARRIGUES WALKER, JOAQUÍN; politically oriented son of elder statesman Antonio Garrigues Díaz-Cañabate; left the management of his family's financial affairs to become the leader of a small Liberal political party and minister of public works in the King's third government.

GIRÓN, JOSÉ ANTONIO; ex-minister of considerable influence with Franco; helped persuade Franco that the Spirit of February 12 was going too far.

GONZÁLEZ MÁRQUEZ, FELIPE; thirty-seven-year-old leader of the Spanish

Socialist Workers Party (PSOE); led his party from illegality in the Franco years to the second position of political party strength in Spain in the June 15, 1977 elections; in the process established himself as not only a national but also an international figure.

GUERRA, ALFONSO; Felipe González's immediate deputy in the PSOE and intimate friend from Sevilla.

GUTIÉRREZ MELLADO, GENERAL MANUEL; an army officer who favored political liberalization and in whom the King had great confidence; one of the King's tutors during his youth; named first vice-president for defense affairs by the King in late 1976.

IBÁÑEZ FREIRE, GENERAL ANTONIO; a military man with experience in civil governorships and as head of the Civil Guard; became minister of interior after the March 1979 legislative elections.

IBARRURI, DOLORES; the famous La Pasionaria of Civil War days and a long-time Spanish Communist Party leader.

INIESTA CANO, CARLOS; a retired right-wing general who wrote an open letter against the legalization of the Spanish Communist Party.

KISSINGER, HENRY; secretary of state during the first three years covered by this book.

LAVILLA ALSINA, LANDELINO; young minister of justice in the King's second cabinet; undersecretary of industry in Franco's last government; his highest previous public position; recognized for his legal talent and attention to detail.

LÓPEZ DE LETONA, JOSÉ MARÍA; minister of industry under Franco; friend of the King whom the King probably considered for the prime ministership.

MARTÍN VILLA, RODOLFO; young and able minister of interior in the King's second cabinet; product of the Franco regime with a labor and ministry of finance background who rose by native ability to be a successful civil governor of Barcelona at the end of the Franco regime; personable, politically astute, and an excellent organizer.

MCCLOSKEY, ROBERT; American career diplomat; led the United States team that negotiated the Treaty of Friendship and Cooperation with Spain.

MONDEJAR, THE MARQUÉS DE; chief of the the King's household and a close advisor to the King for many years.

MÚGICA, ENRIQUE; third in line in the PSOE power structure and a moderate who openly calls himself a Social Democrat.

OREJA AGUIRRE, MARCELINO; a young diplomat, banker, and politician who was Cabanillas's undersecretary and resigned in sympathy with him in October 1974; returned as undersecretary of foreign affairs in the King's first cabinet and became minister of foreign affairs in June 1976.

ORIOL, ANTONIO; president of the Council of State who was kidnapped on December 10, 1976 (he was released unharmed).

OSORIO, ALFONSO; Christian Democratic product of the Franco regime who became the first minister of the presidency under the King.

OTERO NOVAS, JOSÉ MANUEL; a confidant of Suárez who was minister of the presidency after the June 1977 elections and became minister of education after the March 1979 elections.

PÉREZ LLORCA, JOSÉ PEDRO; UCD leader in the Congress of Deputies who was named minister of the presidency after the March 1979 elections.

PIÑAR, BLAS; leader of the extreme Right in Spain.

PITA DA VEIGA, ADMIRAL GABRIEL; minister of the navy in the last Franco government and in the first two governments of the King; resigned over the legalization of the Spanish Communist Party.

RIVERO, ADMIRAL HORACIO; former deputy chief of naval operations; ambassador to Spain at the time of the author's assignment to Spain.

RODRÍGUEZ DE VALCARCEL, ALEJANDRO; conservative who was president of the Cortes during the last years of Franco's life.

RODRÍGUEZ SAHAGÚN, AUGUSTÍN; a businessman who became minister of industry under Suárez and then, after the March 1979 elections, Spain's first civilian minister of defense.

ROVIRA, JUAN JOSÉ; able Spanish career diplomat who was undersecretary of foreign affairs in 1974 and 1975; led the Spanish team that negotiated the renewal (in treaty form) of the US-Spanish agreement on military base facilities; later ambassador to Washington.

RUÍZ GIMÉNEZ, JOAQUÍN; minister in the Franco regime who broke with Franco over the latter's failure to liberalize politically; became a Christian Democratic leader and espouser and defender of liberal causes (he did poorly in the June 15, 1977 elections, however).

RUBIAL, RAMÓN; septuagenarian worker-philosopher who is president of the PSOE.

SÁNCHEZ TERÁN, ENRIQUE; personable ex–civil governor of Barcelona who served as liaison man between the government and Catalán leadership in the negotiations for the reestablishment of the Generalitat and the return of Taradellas; later named minister of transportation.

SANTIAGO Y DÍAZ DE MENDÍVIL, GENERAL FERNANDO DE; conservative army officer who was the King's first vice-president for defense affairs; later resigned in disagreement with the degree of political liberalization that was taking place.

STABLER, WELLS; United States ambassador to Spain from early March 1975 to May 1978.

SUÁREZ GONZÁLEZ, ADOLFO; young politician from the last years of the Franco regime who became, in June 1976, the King's second prime minister and abetted the King in leading the Spanish democratic transition.

TAMAMES, RAMÓN; a left-leaning economist who revealed himself as a member of the Spanish Communist Party's central committee at the July 28, 1976, Rome meeting.

TARADELLAS, JOSEP; elderly Catalán leader in exile for over thirty years who came back to Catalonia in October 1977 as the first president of the Generalitat, Catalonia's traditional governing body.

VEGA RODRÍGUEZ, GENERAL MIGUEL; army chief of staff who resigned in the spring of 1978 because of friction over lines of authority between him and First Vice-President for Defense Affairs General Manuel Gutiérrez Mellado.

VILLAESCUSA, EMILIO; president of the Supreme Military Justice Council who was kidnapped on January 24, 1977, and later released unharmed as the result of a successful police operation.

VILLAR MIR, JUAN MIGUEL; minister of finance in the King's first government who was not successful in dealing with Spain's deteriorating economic situation.

SPANISH
CONSTITUTIONS C

THE HISTORICAL BACKGROUND

The Office of Diplomatic Information of the Spanish Ministry of Foreign
Affairs has provided the following brief history of Spanish constitutions.

The history of Spanish constitutions begins in 1812. Since that time,
Spain has had seven constitutions all told, including the one which has
just been adopted by the Spanish people in a referendum. We do not
include in this total the Statute of Bayonne, sanctioned in 1808 by
Joseph I, which many authors are reluctant to regard as a constitution
because it was imposed by force as a result of the Napoleonic invasion.

Consequently, the first Spanish Constitution is the one promulgated
in Cadiz on March 19th, 1812. It is a liberally inspired Constitution,
drawing heavily on classical Spanish thought and also influenced by the
French Declaration of 1791. It was taken as a basis for the drafting of
many South American constitutions in the 19th century. In it, sovereignty
was declared to reside in the nation, in the form of a restricted heredi-
tary constitutional monarchy. It established the separation of the three
powers and stipulated that Catholicism should be the sole state religion.
It guaranteed freedom of the press and of opinion and a wide range of
individual rights. The Cortes constituted the only chamber, as a national
assembly with unity of representation, both quantitive and proportional.
It lay with the King to sanction and promulgate laws. He also had a
restricted right of suspensive veto. The Constitution of Cádiz was in
force from March 19th to May 4th 1812, and during the periods 1820–
23 and 1836–37. In 1834, although the Crown had issued a Royal
Statute after the death of King Ferdinand VII, this cannot really be
considered a Constitution.

The next Constitution, that of 1837, was a liberal document, which
maintained the basic principle of sovereignty residing in the nation and

of the rights of the individual already expressed in its predecessor. However, this time Catholicism was not made the official state religion; Catholicism was simply said to be the de facto existing religion among the Spanish people. The Constitution of 1837 strengthened royal power and established the bicameral system, comprising the Senate and the Congress of Deputies. The Senate was a conservative chamber, which was only renewed by thirds, which gave it its stable character.

The Constitution of 1845, which followed a period of civil warfare, reaffirmed the power of the Executive over the Cortes, which continued to be bicameral. However, Congress lost its chief powers and it was the Senate, made up of notables favorable to the Crown, that undertook the bulk of the legislation. At the same time, individual rights were curtailed and the State was defined as a Catholic one once more.

In the mid-19th century, the personalistic behaviour of the Executive became more pronounced, which brought about, in 1854, a two-year progressive period, which drafted a new Constitution, which was never proclaimed. After this brief hiatus, the conservative text of 1845 continued in force until 1869.

After the progressive revolution of 1868, Spanish history saw a new Constitution of a markedly liberal kind, which remained in force until 1873. The text was based on the ideas of constitutional monarchy and the sovereignty of the nation. The Constitution of 1869 included a long list of human rights (freedom of press, teaching, worship, assembly, association, right to vote, etc.). The bicameral system was maintained, with an equal number of deputies and senators. The King could dissolve Cortes, but they had to be summoned anually. The Constitution was obliged to face the new social and political phenomena of the time, including the rise of socialism, anarchism, and federalism.

As a response to the federalism which inspired the proclamation of the Monarchy, a new Constitution was adopted. The State became confessional once more, although the practice of other religions was allowed. Sovereignty was shared between the Cortes and the Monarchy. The King acquired new powers and Congress and Senate were renewed every five years. The Senate was made up as follows: 180 senators were elected by State corporations and by the biggest taxpayers; and the rest were renewed every five years. It was a moderate Constitution, which accepted part of the preceding reforms without relinquishing a high degree of conservatism. It remained in force until 1923, when the dictatorship of General Primo de Rivera began.

In 1931, the 2nd Spanish Republic was proclaimed. Its first task was to draft a new Constitution, which drew its inspiration basically from those of 1812 and 1869 and reflected the ideological and social concerns of Spain in the first third of the 20th century. Its first article defined the State as a democratic Republic of workers of all kinds. Its chief novelties were the acceptance of autonomous communities within the single unified State and the inclusion of social, economic and labour

FIGURE C-1

Spanish Constitutions and Their Characteristics

Constitutions	Sovereignty Resides In	Ideological Character	Relation of Powers	Reformability	Actual Framer of Constitution	In Force
1812	Nation	Progressive	Recognizes separation of powers	Very rigid	Constituent Cortes	5 or 6 years (not consecutive)
Statute 1834	King	Conservative	No separation of powers	Flexible	King by royal decree	3 years
1837	Nation	Progressive	Recognizes collaboration of powers	Flexible	Constituent Cortes	8 years
1845	King and Cortes	Conservative	No separation of powers	Flexible	Reform 1837 Constitution	24 years
1869	Nation	Progressive	Recognizes separation of powers	Rigid	Constituent Cortes	4 years
1876	King and Cortes	Conservative	No separation of powers	Flexible	Constituent Cortes	47 years
1931	People	Progressive	Collaboration of powers	Rigid	Constituent Cortes	8 years
Laws 1938–67	Indeterminate: Head of State, Cortes, Nation	Conservative	Unity of power	Very rigid	General Franco	37 years
Constitution 1978	People	Progressive	Collaboration of powers	Very rigid	Constituent Cortes	

rights which made it one of the most progressive texts of its time. The Cortes, which elected the president of the nation, consisted of a single chamber, the depository of popular sovereignty. Suffrage was universal, direct, equal and secret. According to the experts, the Spanish Constitution of 1931 attempted to yoke the centrifugal forces of democracy to a strong executive.

The confrontation among the various social forces, which led to the Civil War, put an end to this Constitution, which was repealed in 1939, and gave place to a series of Fundamental Laws which were the basis of the regime of Francisco Franco. At no time did these laws—in the opinion of Professor Duverger—give shape to a Constitution in the formal sense, although as a whole they comprised a legal corpus of a constitutional nature, twice approved by referendum.

Nineteen seventy-eight opens a new constitutional era, which links up with Spanish democratic tradition.

We now give a general outline of the Spanish Constitutions, published in "Patterns in Spanish Constitutionalism, 1908–1976" and completed with the present Constitution by the newspaper *Diario-16*. As may be seen, the table also contains the Statute of 1834 and the Fundamental Laws of Francoism.

THE NEW CONSTITUTION

The following summary of the principal provisions of the 1978 Spanish Constitution has been provided by an expert in the US Department of State.*

> The Spanish Constitution in general sets out the institutional and procedural framework of a typical Western European parliamentary monarchy. But it also has unique features, arising out of Spain's recent and more distant historical past, that include:

1. Repeated and emphatic concern for protecting human rights:
   - These are elaborated, in some detail, in the first of ten titles in the Constitution.
   - They are linked to extra-Hispanic standards, specifically, the Universal Declaration of Human Rights (article 10).
   - They take into account contemporary technological implications, such as wiretapping and data processing (article 18).
   - The mission and responsibilities of the state security forces are described largely in terms of protection of citizens rights (article 104, 105).

---

*J. Ehrman of the Bureau of Intelligence and Research of the Department of State.

2. Reconciliation of historically competing or antagonistic interests:

   - Although there is to be "no state religion," public authorities are to take "the religious beliefs of Spanish society" into account and to maintain "relations of cooperation" with the Catholic Church and other faiths (article 16). The right of parents to provide their children with a religious education is assured (article 27).

   - Free enterprise is recognized "within the framework of a market economy" (article 38); however, the country's wealth, "by whomsoever it may be owned, is subordinate to the general interest" (article 128).

   - The Constitution emphasizes the "indissoluble unity of the Spanish nation, the common and indivisible country of all Spaniards" (article 2); it also serves to protect "all Spaniards and peoples of Spain" (preamble) as well as the "cultural heritage" which the "wealth of ... different language variations" in the country represents (article 3).

   - Along the same lines, Castilian is the official language of Spain, which all Spaniards have "the duty to know," but the other languages of Spain are to enjoy official status in the several self-governing communities.

3. The setting aside of details, as well as potentially thorny issues, for elaboration in organic laws to be developed in parliament:

   - Establishing certain state institutions, such as the Defender of the People (article 54), the Council of State (article 107), the General Council of the Judiciary (article 122), the Court of Audit (article 136), and the Constitutional Court (article 165).

   - Governing the Armed Forces (article 8) and the Security Forces (article 104).

   - Having to do with the creation of Self-Governing Communities (article 144), the transfer of powers to them (article 150), and their rights of taxation (article 157).

   - Stipulating details of the succession to the Crown (article 57), the holding of referendums (articles 87 and 92), and the election of senators (article 69).

The Constitution is also noteworthy in that it:

   - Restores the Monarchy and declares that "the King is the Head of State, the symbol of its unity and permanence" (article 56).

   - Makes it relatively easy for parliament to select a prime minister (article 99) and relatively difficult for it to get rid of him (article 113).

   - Contains elaborate provisions for regional autonomy which, however, may "under no circumstances" give rise to federal arrangements in Spain (articles 143–158).

SELECTED BIBLIOGRAPHY

BOOKS

Alba, Victor. *El Partido Comunista en España*. Barcelona: Editorial Planeta, 1979. A thorough study of the Spanish Communist Party.

Areilza, José María de. *Diario de un Ministro de la Monarquía*. Barcelona: Editorial Planeta, 1977. An interesting firsthand account of events during the time of the King's first government, from December 1975 to July 1976, written by the foreign minister in that government.

Armero, José Mario. *La Política Exterior de Franco*. Barcelona: Editorial Planeta, 1978. A view of Spanish foreign policy by a Spanish lawyer, newspaperman, and a president of a news agency (Europa Press), who knew most of the principal protagonists personally.

Bardavio, Joaquín. *El Dilema*. Madrid: Strips Editores, 1978. A newspaperman's account of the first months of King Juan Carlos I's reign and of the anatomy of his decision to appoint Adolfo Suárez as prime minister.

Carr, Raymond. *Spain 1808–1939*. Oxford: Clarendon Press, 1966. A competent history.

Carrillo, Santiago. *"Eurocomunismo" y Estado*. Barcelona: Editorial Planeta, 1977. An evocative explanation of so-called Eurocommunism.

Herr, Richard. *Spain*. Berkeley (Calif.): University of California Press, 1974. A scholarly and perceptive work.

Jackson, Gabriel. *The Spanish Republic and the Civil War*. Princeton (NJ): Princeton University Press, 1965. A good account of the Civil War.

Jordan, David C. *Spain, the Monarchy and the Atlantic Community*. Cambridge (Mass.) and Washington (DC): Institute for Foreign Policy Analysis, 1979.

Linz, Juan. "Europe's Southern Frontier: Evolving Trends Toward What?" *Daedalus*, winter 1979.

Menges, Constantine Christopher. *Spain: The Struggle for Democracy Today*. Center for Strategic and International Studies, Georgetown University, The Washington Papers, vol. 2, no. 58. Beverly Hills and London: Sage Publishers, 1978.

Payne, Stanley G. *The Spanish Revolution*. New York: W. W. Norton, 1970. An excellent account.

Thomas, Hugh. *The Spanish Civil War*. New York: Harper & Row, 1961. A standard work on the Civil War.

Vizcaino Casas, Fernando, ... *Y al Tercer Año, Resuscitó*. Barcelona: Editorial Planeta, 1978. An enjoyable spoof on what would happen if Franco were to return.

PERIODICALS

ABC. Traditional Madrid conservative newspaper with good contacts in the establishment.

Cambio 16. Highly successful news magazine that continually tested the limits of the permissible in political commentary during the early transition period.

El País. A newer, more aggressive Madrid newspaper of the Center Left. Tends to take an opposition line.

Vanguardia. Excellent, highly professional Barcelona newspaper.

YA. Outstanding Madrid centrist-oriented newspaper with perhaps Spain's top political columnist in Luis Apostúa, whose short daily column combines an excellent record of principal political events with thoughtful commentary.

INDEX

Abril Martorell, Fernando, 42–43, 57
Acoca, Miguel, 126
Alba, Victor, 71
Alfonso XIII, King, 34
Allende, Salvador, 77
Alvárez de Miranda, Fernando, 42, 51
Apostúa, Luis, 43
Arafat, Yasser, 152
Arias Navarro, Carlos, 8–11 *passim*,
    29–32 *passim*, 36–44, 49, 58–59,
    85, 110, 114, 136, 147–48
Arias Salgado, Rafael, 68
Azcárate, Manuel, 73

Barrera Irimo, Antonio, 9, 58
Berlinguer, Enrico, 46, 149
Bernstein, Eduard, 80
Brandt, Willy, 45, 111, 148
Brown, George S., 18
Byne, Arthur, 25
Byne, Mrs. Arthur, 25
Byrd, Robert, 131

Cabanillas, Pío, 8–9, 29, 51, 58, 103,
    147
Caldwell, Ray, 147n
Calvo Ortega, Rafael, 151
Calvo Sotelo, José, 104

Calvo Sotelo, Leopoldo, 42, 52, 104,
    144
Camacho, Marcelino, 46, 62
Camuñas, Ignacio, 57n
Cantarero, Manuel, 51–52
Carlos III, King, 87
Carrero Blanco, Luis, 3, 7, 32, 85,
    136, 147
Carrillo, Santiago, 45–47, 50, 60,
    66–68, 71–80, 90, 110, 130, 135,
    143–51 *passim*
Carter, Jimmy, 118, 125
Ceausescu, Nicolae, 47, 152
Clark, Kenneth, 73
Clark, Robert, 24
Clavero Arévalo, Manuel, 103
Cortina Mauri, Pedro, 17, 22–23, 35
Cruz Cuenca, Miguel, 99
Cubillo, Antonio, 113
Cunhal, Alvaro, 77

de Araluce, Juan María, 44
de Arana Goiri, Sabino, 88
de Areilza, José María, 23, 31–33
    passim, 37–42 *passim*, 51–54 *passim*,
    57n, 98–101 *passim*, 108–14 *passim*,
    132, 148, 165
de Borbón, Don Juan, 7, 31, 55, 150

de Borbón, Juan Carlos, King, 7–10,
  19, 23–34 *passim*, 38–43 *passim*,
  47–49, 53–66 *passim*, 82–86 *passim*,
  93, 133–41 *passim*, 148
de Borbón, Sofía, 19, 34
de Borchgrave, Arnaud, 38
de Sá Carneiro, Francisco, 68
de Santiago y Díaz de Mendivil,
  Fernando, 33, 42, 47, 148
de Yrizas, Pedro, 88
Diez Alegría, Manuel, 3, 9, 47
Don Juan, *see* de Borbón, Don Juan

Eagleton, Thomas, 24

Felipe, Prince, 34, 35
Ferdinand VII, King, 142, 159
Fernández Miranda, Torcuato, 32–33,
  38, 40, 42, 67, 150
Fernández Ordoñez, Francisco, 9, 51,
  57, 60, 62, 102, 104, 144
Flanagan, Peter, 119–20
Fontán Pérez, Antonio, 103
Ford, Gerald, 11, 147
Fraga Irribarne, Manuel, 10, 29, 33,
  37–42 *passim*, 50–54, 68, 98,
  148–50 *passim*
Franco, Francisco, 1–17 *passim*, 22–31
  passim, 35–39, 85–91 *passim*, 104,
  111–19 *passim*, 128–40 *passim*,
  147–48, 162
Frei, Eduardo, 68
Fuentes Quintana, Enrique, 42, 57,
  60–61

Galván, Tierno, 67, 101
Garaicoechea, Carlos, 20
Garcia Añoveros, Jaime, 103
Garrigues, Antonio, 33, 42, 148
Garrigues Walker, Joaquin, 51
Girón, José Antonio, 9
Giscard d'Estaing, Valéry, 110–11
Gómez Llorente, Luis, 105
González López, Germán, 107

González Márquez, Felipe, 44, 50–52
  passim, 67, 80–82, 98, 105, 111,
  143–46 *passim*, 150–52
Gramsci, Antonio, 72
Gromyko, Andrei, 152
Guerra, Alfonso, 82
Gutiérrez Mellado, Manuel, 19, 33,
  47–48, 57, 64–66, 92, 102, 129, 148

Haddad, Jesús, 151
Hartman, Arthur, 18
Hassan, King of Morocco, 35, 112
Hearst, William Randolph, 25
Hemingway, Ernest, 1, 30
Herrera Tejador, Francisco, 53
Hoffer, Eric, 81
Huntington, Samuel, 142–43

Ibáñez Freire, Antonio, 102
Ibarruri, Dolores, "La Pasionaria,"
  46, 150
Iglesias, Pablo, 80
Iniesta Cano, Carlos, 47

John XXIII, Pope, 134

Khrushchev, Nikita, 75
Kissinger, Henry, 22–23, 27, 35, 117,
  120, 126–27

Lamó de Espinosa, Jaime, 151
Largo Caballero, Francisco, 80
Lavilla, Landelino, 42, 67, 103–4, 144
Lemos, William, 17
Lenin, V. I., 67, 72, 80
Linz, Juan, 165
Llanteno, Viscount of, 25
López de Letona, José María, 32, 39

Marchais, Georges, 46, 149
Martín Gamero, Adolfo, 42
Martín Villa, Rodolfo, 42, 93, 101–2,
  104, 144

Marx, Karl, 72, 80–81
McCloskey, Robert, 22
McNeil, Frank, 54
Menges, Constantine Christopher, 4–5, 165
Miláns de Bosch, Jaime, 107
Mitterrand, François, 45, 148
Mondéjar, Marqués de, 32
Múgica, Enrique, 82–83

Nenni, Pietro, 45, 148
Nixon, Richard, 119

Oreja, Marcelino, 9, 19, 42–43, 111, 114, 132, 150, 151, 152
Oriol, Antonio, 44, 148, 149
Ortín Gil, Constantino, 92, 99
Osorio, Alfonso, 33, 39, 42, 57, 67, 98, 101
Otero Novas, José Manuel, 103
Owen, David, 111, 150, 151

Palme, Olaf, 45, 148
Pérez-Llorca, José Pedro, 103
Piñar, Blas, 91
Pita da Veiga, Gabriel, 48, 149
Poniatowski, Michel, 68
Primo de Rivera, Miguel, 25, 160

Rivero, Horacio, 9, 16, 21, 119–20
Robles Piquer, Carlos, 42
Rodríguez de Valcárcel, Alejandro, 30, 32

Rodríguez Sahagún, Agustín, 102, 151
Rovira, Juan José, 22
Rubial, Ramón, 81
Ruiz, Mariana, 5
Ruiz Giménez, Joaquín, 51–52
Rumor, Mariano, 68

Sánchez, Valentín, 5
Sánchez Terán, Enrique, 63, 151
Solzhenitsyn, Aleksandr, 6
Stabler, Wells, 17–18, 120, 127, 132
Stalin, J., 12, 75
Suárez, Adolfo, 10, 19, 26, 33, 40–68 passim, 92, 96–103 passim, 110–12 passim, 131–34, 141–50 passim, 165

Tamames, Ramón, 46
Taradellas, Josep, 63
Tarancón, see Vicente Tarancón
Thatcher, Margaret, 68
Thomas, Hugh, 166
Thorn, Gaston, 68
Tindemans, Leo, 68
Todman, Terence, 132

Vance, Cyrus, 18, 114
Vega Rodríguez, Miguel, 65
Vergara, Juan, 4
Vicente Tarancón, Enrique, 140
Villaescusa, Emilio, 44, 64, 149
Villar Mir, Juan Miguel, 59–60
Viola Sauret, Joaquín, 151
Vizcaíno Casas, Fernando, 7n, 166